Sutapa Biswas

Other inIVA monographs include:

Avtarjeet Dhanjal
Keith Piper: Relocating the Remains
Aubrey Williams
Shen Yuan
Li Yuan-chia: tell me what is not yet said

To place an order, visit www.iniva.org or
email: booksales@iniva.org

Sutapa Biswas

Institute of International Visual Arts, London,
in collaboration with the Douglas F. Cooley
Memorial Art Gallery, Reed College,
Portland, Oregon

Published in the United Kingdom by the
Institute of International Visual Arts (inIVA)
in collaboration with the Douglas F. Cooley
Memorial Art Gallery, Reed College,
Portland, Oregon

Institute of International
Visual Arts
6-8 Standard Place
Rivington Street
London EC2A 3BE
www.iniva.org

© 2004 inIVA
Texts © 2004 the authors
Images © 2004 Sutapa Biswas,
unless otherwise stated

Edited by Sarah Campbell
Designed by Untitled

Production co-ordinated
by Uwe Kraus GmbH
Printed in Italy

Published on the occasion of *Sutapa
Biswas: Birdsong*, an inIVA touring
exhibition produced in collaboration with
Film and Video Umbrella. Supported by
Arts Council England Grants for National
Touring, AHRB, Chelsea College of Art and
Design (University of the Arts, London),
the Culture Company and the University
of Southampton.

Cafe Gallery Projects
Southwark Park, London
26 May – 20 June 2004

Angel Row Gallery
Nottingham
18 September – 6 November 2004

Harewood House
Leeds
2 October – 14 November 2004

Leeds City Art Gallery
2 October – 14 November 2004

Douglas F. Cooley
Memorial Art Gallery
Reed College, Portland, Oregon
September – November 2005

Every effort has been made to trace
copyright holders, but if any have
inadvertently been overlooked, the
publishers will be pleased to make
the necessary arrangements at the
first opportunity.

ISBN 1-899846-39-5

A catalogue record of this book is
available from the British Library.

On the front cover: *Birdsong*, 2004.
16mm film. Photograph: Toby Glanville.

ARTS COUNCIL ENGLAND

UNIVERSITY OF THE ARTS
LONDON

Contents

Foreword
Gilane Tawadros, Director, inIVA

Looking across more than two decades of her distinctive artistic practice, there is one continuous and recurring subject matter that emerges forcefully from Sutapa Biswas's work: time. Not linear time that moves sequentially from beginning to end. Nor present time, unhinged from the past. Time, in Biswas's work, is fleeting and elusive and yet capable of changing everything irrevocably, over and over again. The fragile, metallic birds in her most recent film, *Magnesium Bird*, are ignited and metamorphose before our eyes, almost beyond recognition. The small boy who sits waiting, staring expectantly out towards the camera in *Birdsong*, awaits a magical happening that transforms his immediate, everyday world. In these works, Biswas's lens captures a quality of time and light that finds echoes in the great paintings of Vermeer, Stubbs and Hopper. From her earliest paintings of the 1980s through to her more recent film works, Biswas has been preoccupied with the search to push representation beyond the secure confines of describing the physical world to embody the pleasure and pain of lived experience. In these new works, Biswas takes this search further to produce poetic works that are magical and compelling.

This monograph accompanies an exhibition of newly commissioned works by Sutapa Biswas that confirm her place as one of the most significant artists of her generation. Emerging in Britain in the 1980s when searching questions around race, gender and representation were being most powerfully articulated by a new generation of black British artists, she has consistently challenged the prescribed conventions and limits of both race and representation.

There are so many people without whom Biswas's two new films and this accompanying publication would not have been possible. I would like to thank all those at Film and Video Umbrella (in particular Bevis Bowden); our copublishers, Reed College, and Stephanie Snyder's enthusiasm to show Biswas's work in the US; Sarah Brown of The Culture Company who programme Harewood House; Magnesium Elektron; Bob Hollow Special Effects; Deborah Dean at Angel Row and Ron Henocq at Cafe Gallery Projects for their early commitment to the project; inIVA's staff (especially David A. Bailey, Sarah Campbell, Bruce Haines and Lissa Kinnaer); all the writers for their thoughtful and considered insight into Biswas's work; and all those who have generously lent images for the book. And, most importantly, we are immensely grateful to Sutapa Biswas for her extraordinary energy and commitment to the project and, above all, her unique artistic vision.

Birds and flower motifs on one of the artist's sari.

An Exchange: In Conversation with Sutapa Biswas

Stephanie Snyder, Director, Douglas F. Cooley Memorial Art Gallery, Reed College

I first encountered the work of Sutapa Biswas on a very quiet Thursday afternoon at the Tate Modern, London. On a small video monitor a 'moving image' didn't really move at all, swaying only slightly, the light subtly shifting. The imagery was arresting. In a rather English-looking drawing room, a middle-aged, pot-bellied man stood naked, at a three-quarters angle to the viewer, contemplatively gazing out of a large window into a gentle sunlight that poured over the man's pale body. The more I studied the imagery, the more familiar it seemed. Where had I seen it before? And then it occurred to me that although I was thousands of miles from home, I was gazing at a work based on an Edward Hopper painting. The melancholy ennui of the man's posture in front of the window felt so quintessentially American that I found myself questioning the work's motives. Why was a female, Indian-born British artist appropriating American paintings in a more compelling way than I had ever seen by an American artist? I was intrigued if not smitten. Years later (in 2003) I discovered that inIVA (Institute of International Visual Arts) was co-producing a new body of Biswas's film work, produced this time in sumptuous 16mm. I contacted inIVA and discussions began that led to the Cooley Art Gallery's participation in this monograph and in bringing Sutapa Biswas and her work to Reed College. It has been a rich and gratifying process and I am grateful to inIVA, and particularly to Sutapa Biswas, for the opportunity to delve into her work and her process. The following exchange began on 4 January 2004 at Biswas's home in London – that first twelve-hour conversation left us both hoarse – and continued the following day at inIVA's offices.

Stephanie Snyder＿Let's begin by examining your most recent 16mm film pieces. We are looking at an image from *Birdsong* (2004), your large-scale film installation piece partially inspired by British painter George Stubbs' 1759 work *Lord Holland and Lord Albemarle Shooting at Goodwood*. In making this piece, you began by completely transforming a derelict house into a temporal and physical hybrid of a late eighteenth-century estate and your own home. The objects and references in this image are numerous, but to try and describe the scene simply: in a formal drawing room bathed in sunlight, a young boy (of obviously Indian origin) sits on a couch. In front of him stands a chestnut horse dressed in Portuguese saddle. About the room are furnishings and objects from various time periods – objects as diverse as

08

Above left: Edward Hopper,
A Woman in the Sun, 1961.
Oil on canvas, 101.92 x 155.58cm.
Whitney Museum of American Art,
New York; 50th Anniversary Gift of
Mr and Mrs Albert Hackett in honour
of Edith and Lloyd Goodrich 84.31.
Photograph: Bill Jacobson.

Above right: *The Trials and Tribulations
of Mickey Baker* (detail), 1997.
Video projection. Still.

contemporary children's toys, eighteenth- and
nineteenth-century small-scale statuary, stacks of
literature, and an Oriental carpet. Can you describe
the process of transforming the space?
Sutapa Biswas__I have my sketchbook, where I have
kept an entire record of the process of creating this
piece. I began with colour, which is very important to
me and so in my sketchbook I keep paint swatches
known as heritage sheets.
SS__Eighteenth- and nineteenth-century traditional
English colours – the colours of empire. Are the colours
directly appropriated from the Stubbs painting?
SB__The colours of empire, indeed. I worked from
the colour scheme in the Stubbs painting. For me
the important intersections of colour and meaning
were: the red and yellow/ochre of the young servants'
outfits and of course the green of the landscape.
I matched these as closely as I could to the heritage
paint colours. The Stubbs painting was a starting
point, but by intersecting with the painting as a
historical object, the process went far beyond that.
We went through great pains to actually locate period
objects reproduced in the heritage catalogues.
SS__How did you go about finding the objects and
the raw space?

SB__We went to a location finder and in a sense
searched for somebody who was willing to let a horse
into his or her living room. We eventually found a home
in High Wycombe, which is just outside of London.
The house has a very sad story attached to it. It's a
1930–40s Art Deco house that is about to be pulled
down by the property developer who currently owns it.
It was a threadbare room, in very poor condition.
SS__In your process of developing elaborate sets,
there's an overlap with more traditional methods of
film-making and other time-based, video installation
work. Would you speak about this aspect of *Birdsong*
and of your work in general?
SB__I worked from the basis of my own domestic
space, but trying to work sympathetically with the
nature of the room, which, as an empty space, didn't
really have very much that was appealing, apart from
the grandness of its scale. I wanted it to look like a
grandparent's house that belonged to both this world
and another.
SS__Also, you inserted contemporary objects into
your historical 're-creation' and some of the objects,
like the toy plastic sailing ship and the books, belong
to your son and to you. The toys and the literary works
– by Tolstoy, Borges, Walcott, Proust and Robert Louis

Stevenson to name a few – are contemporary editions of historical objects. They bring home the reality that, in examining history, we are bound to do so through the imagination of the present.

SB__They are contemporary objects that reference the past. It's also interesting that the toy ship is Captain Hook's pirate ship from *Peter Pan*; it's a mythical object, a ship that we find in Never Land. I thought it was necessary to have contemporary objects in that space because I didn't want to create nostalgia for a bygone era. Instead, I wanted to bridge timeframes and spaces while allowing a temporal disruption to happen through my son's toys.

SS__Reframing the history of art in relation to cultural theory is a traditionally postmodern strategy – if one can use 'traditional' and 'postmodern' in the same sentence. This strategy usually produces art whose social/political and ironic aspects are more transparent and acerbic than what I see in your work. Your practice does not come across as an in-your-face social critique, in contrast to that of Hans Haacke or Adrian Piper, for instance. You seem to approach culture from a more personalised, hybridised dreamlike space, seducing the viewer into considering social and political issues.

SB__I work very instinctively, so my starting point is steeped in an understanding and a knowledge both of particular historical readings and of critical readings around practice and theory. I've been self-conscious in trying to open out semantic spaces in order to allow spillage, in order to engage the viewer with issues around time, around presence and around absence. There is playfulness in my approach to addressing serious issues. In a strange way, they are dream spaces that I create, but they also touch my daily experience. My son Enzo is the boy in *Birdsong*. One of the first things that he said to me as a young child was, 'Mum, I would like to have a horse.' At the time we lived in a flat and when I asked him where he thought he would like the horse to live, he responded by saying, 'In my living room.'

SS__Brilliant. Enzo has informed the piece as much as Stubbs. It's apparent that most adults lose the sense of imaginative play and inversion that we naturally have as children, and that is often such an important aspect of art making.

SB__Yes, and this sense of play is so important. It has driven me, actually. The absolutely ridiculous notion of a horse being in your lived space is insane, but it's no more insane than the story of Peter Pan

10

Tinker Tailor Soldier Sailor, 1994.
Text projection on sail boat, 35mm
slide and timer. Installation shot and
detail, Pitt Rivers Museum, Oxford.

or the work of Edward Lear, or acts of cultural domination.

SS__You have also been very inspired by the work of Edward Lear. *The Owl and the Pussycat* informs your other recent film work *Magnesium Bird* (2004). I'm starting to understand that play functions as an amazing hinge in your work. For instance, in your 1994 installation at the Pitt Rivers Museum in Oxford, *Tinker Tailor Soldier Sailor*, you used children's rhymes to underscore the power of race and class in British society. Play is a rather essential, liberating vehicle for conveying and shifting meaning. I see both of these things happening in your work.

SB__Play makes so many things possible. If you allow that magical dream space to exist, even for a moment, if you get back under the table with a child to play, it makes so much possible. Becoming a mother has been very rewarding in that sense, because it has taken me back to those moments of play. That was important for me, because it took me back to the moment of first arriving in England and encountering the British attitude that children should be seen but not heard. I remember trying to understand, 'Why can't I play? I should be allowed to play.' My father used to say these wonderful words: 'One day the world will

be full of dance, music and play', and so I grew up with his notion of dance, music and play.

SS__Which are certainly so important in Indian culture.

SB__Yes, absolutely. The idea of music and sound being the soul of the body and the idea of playing being akin to dancing are interrelated concepts. They are important to Indian culture, but also to a certain philosophy of life. My father was a well-read man, so his was a sort of utopian vision.

SS__Utopianism can be a very removed position, but I sense that you're not interested in presenting an alternative reality that is so removed and unattainable that one can't relate to it immediately.

SB__I'm not trying to present a utopian reality. I'm more interested in that magical moment of first encounter, when, completely involuntarily, one falls in love with a place. I think one of the most interesting things that came out of empire is that something significant happens when somebody who belongs to one world is transported to another world. I do not want to romanticise or to deproblematise the history of empire, but I think it is really powerful when people experience things for the first time – the way people fall in love with a totally unfamiliar place or a new idea for the first time.

SS__In relation to the ideas of play and dreamscape and sensuality and immersion, what was it like for you when you went back to India for the first time, at the age of twenty-one? Was it like entering a dream world?

SB__That's a really tough question, because it was both familiar and unfamiliar, and overwhelming really. I arrived in Delhi, where the landscape has a desert-like quality which is really quite different from the exquisite and beautiful green landscape of Santiniketan, in West Bengal, which is where I was born. Landing at Delhi airport, the heat was very prevalent. Some things were familiar. Smells to an extent were familiar; the colours were familiar; I think the volume of bodies was somehow familiar. And the sounds were incredibly familiar, particularly the sound of the whistle blown by the local watchmen in the mornings.

SS__Do you have strong memories from your childhood in Bengal?

SB__I do, and they have surfaced in unusual ways. While in India, I was at my grandmother's house, and I was taken right back to childhood. I travelled with a friend, who needed to use the bathroom during the night. Because she wasn't able to communicate with my aunt and my grandmother in Bengali, they woke me up. I was convinced that I was three or two years of age and was being woken up in the middle of the night to make a visit to the bathroom and so I responded by saying, 'I don't want to go to the toilet, I don't need to go to the toilet.' That sense of travelling back in time was a strange moment and it left me feeling very disconcerted. I was so transformed back to a particular state in my mind's eye. Returning to India, there were things that were familiar, such as the school where my brother and sister went. Even though a large part of the area surrounding that district has been deforested for economic reasons – sadly – the quality of the light there was very recognisable to me.

SS__Quality of light, that's something that we definitely need to talk about. You are, I would say, obsessed, fascinated and intimately concerned with light in your work.

SB__Yes, I think that's very true. Even in the context of the room where we shot *Birdsong*, there's an overwhelming presence of light, and it's a very special light. We shot the film right through the day, but in the final film edit we chose a particular intensity and quality of light that delineates a very specific time in the day. And that time is morning. Morning and dusk for me are very important moments; they're magic hours, actually.

SS__They are liminal times.

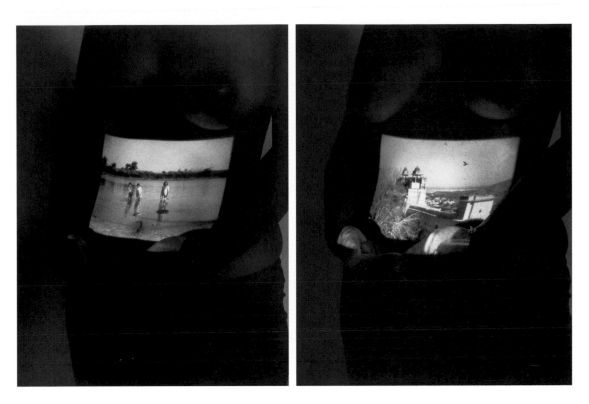

Above left: *Synapse 1*, one, 1992.
Black and white photograph
(five-part work), 112.2 x 132.5cm,
Oldham City Art Gallery Collection, UK.

Above right: *Synapse 1*, five, 1992.
Black and white photograph
(five-part work), 112.2 x 132.5cm,
Oldham City Art Gallery Collection, UK.

Overleaf: *Synapse II*, 1991–92.
Black and white photographs
(two-part work). 112 x 130cm each.

SB__Liminal times – that's exactly right – and it's certainly something that draws me to certain artists' work, in particular Edward Hopper and Johannes Vermeer.
SS__Can you say more about the representation of light in Hopper or Vermeer and the quality of light in your work? Historically, in painting and literature or liturgy, the representation of light signalled also the transmission of knowledge and represented non-verbal, essential experiences such as the impregnation of the Virgin Mary in the Annunciation.
SB__One of the films that I first fell in love with is Michael Powell's 1947 *Black Narcissus*, ironically made at Pinewood Studios outside London, but set in the foothills of the Himalayas in a convent. It's a film that focuses on the relationship between light, religion, empire and hate. Light is so interesting because it is so evocative; you can't transcribe it into words. There's an extraordinary significance in how artists through the centuries have used light both metaphorically and symbolically. And in terms of Vermeer's paintings, which I find so profound and beautiful, light has the most gentle and strange presence in the spaces that he creates. It is something that you can almost literally feel. And I don't know whether somewhere in my

mind's eye his work transports me to a place which is about the heat of light. In *Synapse* (1992), for example, when I projected those images on to my body, I felt that the light from the projector was burning through my skin.
SS__Imprinting upon you.
SB__Yes. And I think that somehow light imprints its presence upon your body.
SS__I can see how your body projections in *Synapse* mirror the idea of light as an impregnating force.
SB__Yes, it is also a reference to the Annunciation. I think that in my *Infestations of the Aorta – Shrine to a Distant Relative* (1989) there also exists a sort of ecclesiastical presence that filters through and penetrates, in the same way that in many religious works of art God's presence penetrates the clouds and bridges heaven and earth. And yet, that aside, there is something about light that is connected to the experience of memory and place. The degree of light, the particular type of light, is something that I associate with place, with moment. Vermeer's *Woman in Blue Reading a Letter* (c. 1662–63) always transports me to that moment when, as a child, I remember looking at my mother reading letters she'd received from India, bathed in light from a window.

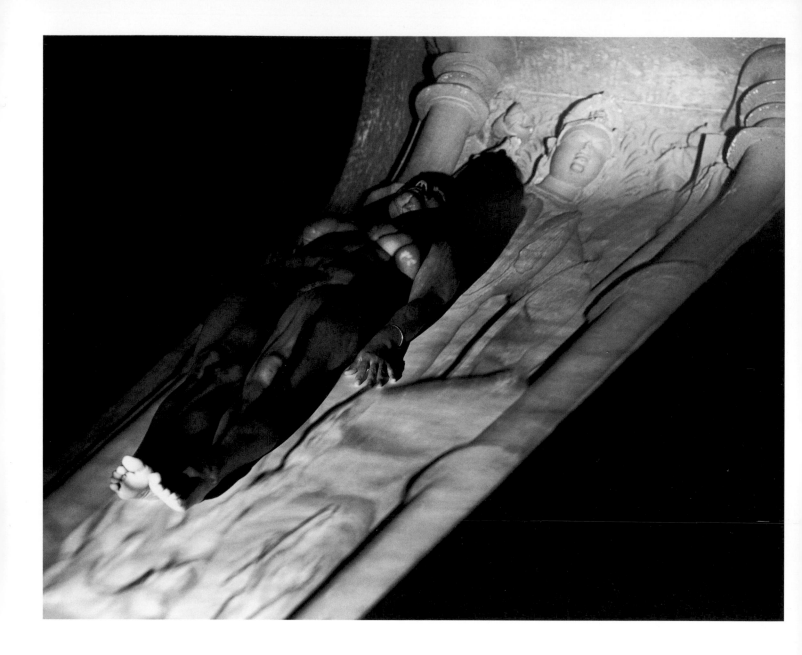

We came to Britain a year after my father left India, travelling by ship for nearly three weeks across water; during the journey, the only light that we experienced, by and large because my mother was so afraid to take us on to deck, was through the porthole.

SS__Which frames experience and light much like a painting.

SB__Absolutely. In fact, I'm doing some initial research around the idea of the porthole for my next film project. I think that particular qualities of light from my early experiences have probably had a very deep impact on me. I discover these experiences in other works of art. In Hopper's work, light penetrates the physicality of the buildings in a way that is extremely disturbing, but also very beautiful. There's something very melancholy in Hopper's paintings, which is a quality I also find in Vermeer's work.

SS__Before melancholia became a clinical disorder, it was a spiritual, metaphysical necessity. It was an important mental/emotional facility and an action of devotion.

SB__Yes and maybe light is so important because it lays things bare and makes people vulnerable, revealing deep emotions. Light exposes the lines, the curves, the moles, the freckles – all of those things that are actually quite beautiful. As a child, I remember really studying somebody's face in a way that verged on rudeness in how much I stared. As adults we learn not to stare, not to study, because somehow it's considered an invasion of privacy.

SS__Although you are a film-maker, the light that you aim for in your work is not a technological or an artificial light; it is a natural light entering from an oblique angle, which offers up the subject of your work as an object of contemplation.

SB__Yes, and it even invites the viewer in, offering them an experience of intimate contemplation. It is a very consistent element in my work. I'm almost astounded at how much it carries through from the very earliest work right through to the most recent pieces.

SS__I'd like to segue into discussing the relationship in your work between visuality and language, specifically poetry – thinking about the ways that you dialogue with word, image and also sound. You use film in such a quiet painterly way.

SB__That's a good point. It's an interesting thing, because with light, try as you might, it can fall on you but you can't catch it. You can represent how it falls and filters but if you try and hold it, there's nothing in

Scenes from *Alice in Wonderland*, as spied through the viewfinder of a small toy that the artist has owned since the age of six.

16

essence to hold on to; instead, it holds you. And I think that it's the same quality that I find very beautiful in poetry. As you read poetry, the sounds that you make in reciting or reading it in your mind's eye produce liminal spaces where, in between the word which is spoken and the word which is suggested, there is a whole other world that lives just at that point of juncture.

SS__One of Derrida's ideas that I find intriguing is the idea of *différance*. I'm going to over-simplify, but, basically, it's the idea that linguistic meaning is always splintering off, deferring, suggesting and pointing to other possibilities.

SB__And I love that; I find it very seductive. I find it immensely pleasurable to watch how language turns itself over, splinters, and divides. Edward Lear's *The Owl and the Pussycat* is about the most unlikely creatures falling in love and disappearing for a year and a day, not just a year, but a year and a day.

SS__And you're going to be dialoguing with *The Owl and the Pussycat* in *Magnesium Bird*?

SB__Yes. In between the actual words of Lear's poem, there is so much nonsense, so much spinning and turning and splintering that goes on. I love the alchemy of that. The transformations that are possible *through language* are very important to me. I think this is also something that's critical to *Birdsong*, because just as you become familiar with something in the image, you look at something else, and the original association slips away and becomes something else.

SS__Critics have discussed the idea of absence in relation to your work, absence from a more Lacanian perspective – a void. From my perspective, the absences within your work are quickly filled and re-emptied by the work's referential complexity.

SB__In the sense of longing that exists in my work, there is also a presence, and I think that's important. Maybe that's why I love the way that children play. For them there's nothing absent, because if it is absent, they will make it present through their imagination, they will conjure it themselves.

SS__Another way that your work intersects with presence and absence is in relation to the source material of your pieces: the paintings that you address. There are other artists who dialogue with paintings through their video work, though not many as far as I know. Bill Viola comes to mind. I just saw *Bill Viola: The Passions* at the National Gallery (London, 2003) and it seems that Viola is interested in building a more straightforward emotional and spiritual bridge to the original work of art.

Murmur, 1993. Video still.

SB__Whereas it is never my intention simply to reference a painting. I'm more interested in moving the dialogue forward.

SS__In a recent *Art Monthly* article about utopianism, Marcus Verhagen asks what's happened to the art that's being made that offers the viewer a better world, a better future.[01] I think that part of what your work does is offer the viewer a window through which to consider other possible worlds: through play, through imagination, through interventions into the past.

SB__That's a beautiful thought. I think if the viewer can come away with something so optimistic that would be wonderful. When Enzo first said to me that he wanted a horse to live in the living room, I felt that, as his mother, it was incumbent upon me to make the impossible happen. Filming *Birdsong* encapsulated a moment of intense beauty, but there was also an intense danger in having a live horse in such confined proximity to Enzo. Combined with the pleasure of the experience, was also a mother's worst fear of losing a child. I remember listening to a documentary about Rudyard Kipling and about his grief when he lost first his daughter and then his son. Some people claim that he was just so grief-stricken that he subsequently died of a broken heart.

SS__Empathy is an interesting word to examine in relation to your work.

SB__And something that, whether it's through music or through prose or poetry, has the most extraordinary ability to allow you to experience something. And there's a kind of empathetic optimism, I think, about poetry, because it doesn't fill in all the spaces; it leaves you to fill in some of those spaces, which I think is really important.

SS__Back to synapses – semantic meeting places.

SB__I remember writing to Homi Bhabha asking him if he would contribute something for the *Synapse* catalogue and he was excited to learn about my work, because at that time he was working on exactly the same issues – the synaptic space, or liminal space – in his book *The Location of Culture* (1994).

SS__This also reminds me of Stuart Hall's discussion about diasporic identity – that identity is not something that we recover from the past. Instead, it's about the ways in which we position ourselves in relation to the *narratives* of the past.

SB__Yes. And I guess that also relates to the idea of why I don't overtly use text to make a point. I am very aware that I want to leave space for the viewer to translate and to interpret.

Above: Waxwork statue of
Jeremy Bentham (containing his
human remains), situated opposite
Sutapa Biswas's *Untitled (Woman in
Blue Weeping)*, as part of the exhibition
The Visible and the Invisible,
University College, London, 1996.

Above right: *Untitled (Woman in Blue
Weeping)*, installed as part of the
exhibition *The Visible and the Invisible*,
University College, London, 1996.

Note
01__Marcus Verhagen, 'Micro-Utopianism',
Art Monthly, no. 272, December 2003,
pp. 1–4.

SS__Intellectually it puts the viewer in a very trusted position. We've discussed the importance of language in relation to your work, and yet your pieces do not have audio tracks. They are silent. I want to ask you about that.

SB__It's true, there is an absence of sound in most of my film and video work. On the other hand, there's a piece of mine called *Murmur*, from 1993, a double video piece – a split-screen projection; it's an ephemeral work in which the camera travels through and across a landscape. It's an interesting collage, but it's edited and cut according to and alongside the sound of a heartbeat. The effect is overwhelming.

SS__Yes, I have viewed that piece and it really does create a unique experience. The sound becomes very droning, atmospheric. Like white noise, I could almost feel it cancelling itself out.

SB__I think it was right to have sound for that particular piece because the sound propelled you through the space. But I like the silence in other pieces, because it is just so deafening sometimes.

SS__John Cage says that silence is not an auditory experience; it's a neurological experience.

SB__Yes, it's absolutely the truth. When you see my piece *Untitled (Woman in Blue Weeping)* (1996),

there's no soundtrack. But you do hear her weeping, because neurologically we know, through memory, what the sound of weeping is.

SS__Do you think the absence of associated sound challenges the viewer to rid themselves of their mental soundtracks?

SB__The neurological experience of silence empties the mind, allowing one to keep pushing at the boundaries, at the edges of things. I try to make pieces that people can fall in love with, so that they question issues around longing and love. Love is a synaptic space. I have fallen in love with many works of art. What that does to me as an individual is that it keeps bringing me back in order that I may move forward. I try in my work to use references and objects to transport the viewer somewhere, in order that he or she can move forward to a different place. That's probably why I love Marcel Proust so much, because he a master at this – he sends you back to a precise moment in order to shape your emergence into another.

London, 5 January 2004

Artist's Statement
Sutapa Biswas, 1987

'In most of my work I've tried to trace certain elements within my own cultural history… to use ideas of myth and to rework those ideas to signify, in very crude ways, imperialism. To try and make the viewer aware of the fact that a particular cultural history existed and to try and encourage the viewer to question what happened to that culture. How was it inverted? Where does it fit into the present-day existence of, for instance, black people, whether they're Afro-Caribbean or Asian people living within Britain? I try to link everyday events to things that perhaps are not everyday events like the idea of myth, story, heroes and heroines… to say that we are all goddesses, we are all heroines, we are all gods. And our histories can be within our own hands.'

Brief extract from a much longer interview that was first published in Sandy Nairne, *State of the Art: Ideas & Images in the 1980s*, London: Chatto & Windus, 1987.

Tracing Figures of Presence: Naming Ciphers of Absence Feminism, Imperialism and Postmodernity: The Work of Sutapa Biswas

Griselda Pollock

Sutapa Biswas earned her undergraduate degree in the Department of Fine Art at the University of Leeds. For some readers this statement will immediately signify; for others, it may indicate no more than 'educational background'. This specific department was and is one of the few in a British university to have the practice of fine art within its regimes of academic study. But after the appointment of social historian of art T.J. Clark to the Chair of Fine Art, and continuing after his brief tenure, the department attempted to create a distinctive programme of study by creating a course evenly divided between history/theory and practice/theory. The join between the two 'sides' of the course was created by the interest, held in common by both artists and art historians, in the politicised theorisation of a critique of modernism. Terry Atkinson, Fred Orton, Tim Clark and I forged links (through seminars, crits and lectures) between hitherto separated domains whose boundaries had been systematically policed, supposedly because those boundaries were a necessary condition for the making of ambitious modernist art. Art History worked to provide a critical genealogy of the formation and disintegration of modernism, while contemporary practice in the studios explored modernism's legacies and manufactured a critical practice that, while it was chronologically postmodernist, was not theoretically entirely symptomatic of what we now call postmodernism. Art History – predominantly grounded in historical materialism – insured that theoretical revision proceeded from an understanding of interests, power, domination, exploitation. It stressed that there are important and concrete issues at stake in the challenges mounted to modernism's suspension of the social and the historical as valid referents for art. This sense of the historical is a means to articulate a political project, a naming of interests and an investment in concrete change, rather than a fashionable substitution of ideas. Feminism played a vital part in the historical and political discourses that were developing at Leeds. Its historical perspective aimed at revising the canonical histories of art in order to acknowledge the presence and persistence of women artists over the ages, while the recognition that femininity and creativity were not, as previous ideological formulations had it, incompatible, forced revision to the very practices of art history and criticism, and led to an understanding of the specificity and meaning of women's inscriptions on the texts of culture. The critique and critical revisions of modernist

Housewives with Steak-Knives, 1985. **Oil, acrylic and pastel on paper, 274 x 244cm. Collection of Bradford City Museums and Art Galleries, Cartwright Hall, UK.**

art and art history, which feminism necessitates, were fast becoming the hallmark of the Leeds Department of Fine Art.

There can be no doubt that this academic environment, this conversational community, influenced the development of Sutapa Biswas away from the immensely skilful and professionally accomplished figurative painting she was then producing, towards an ambitious and critical intervention, by means of multimedia presentations, in the field of dominant representations both local to Leeds and on a world scale.

But Sutapa Biswas's presence on the course was also highly influential. It was she who defined the absences in these seemingly radical discourses deriving from Marxism and feminism. It was she who named the imperialism that still structured analyses, and which spoke in undifferentiated terms of class and gender, never acknowledging the issues of race and colonialism. It was her critique that forced us all to acknowledge the Eurocentric limits of the discourses within which we practised. Her challenge was mounted face to face, not at the level of abstract taunts, but by the direct engagement in dialogue of people sharing a space, a space thus assumed by her generosity to be able and willing to enlarge the critical discourse to accommodate the subjects of class, gender and race in their intricate and painful configurations between us and within us. She demanded change; and response was made, and the course then altered. With the question of imperialism and its racist practices no longer repressed, the space of the studio and the lecture theatre had to be made to articulate the pressure of the social and psychic relations that imperialism, as a still-powerful structure, installed in us all. Instead of presenting binary oppositions, Sutapa Biswas's practice as student and as producer of artworks systematically eroded the cliché of accusation, and hence did not induce defensive withdrawal stemming from guilt.

This is the visible in the work she produced as a conclusion to her degree, *Housewives with Steak-Knives* (1985), which uses the space of the paper (in fact several pieces of paper mapped together) to house conflicting images, systems, meanings. At a formal level, the piece knowingly sets white against black by imaging the Hindu goddess Kali, which means black, on white paper. Kali, however, represents the destroyer of evil, and the signification of this mission through blackness directly assaults the

Eurocentric uses of colour coding in the imposition of their self-valuating moralities. The scale of the figure, and her adornment with both knives, flowers and the hand gesture of peace, makes this representation of that which pursues and punishes evil dominate the space of the picture and the space of the viewer. A centralised and frontal figure of a female goddess is not merely a signifier of power, and therefore threatening, but also a signifier of power and therefore *comforting*, because it is an allegorical figure of empowered femininity, the mother, so often wrongly defined in Western patriarchal psychology as the phallic mother. Her power precedes the slightest intimation that the phallus might signify, and the evocation of the maternal as a source of both order and force, of anger and peace, reminds us of an order of meaning other than that which phallocentrism erects with its perpetual divisiveness. The binary opposition and hierarchical ordering of male and female, characteristic of the West, is dislocated by this grand image of female activity and moral purpose who sports a necklace of identifiable male heads, which form a contemporary cast of political miscreants. These represent the evil that must be purged, in contradistinction to the Western projection of evil onto woman, Eve, who must then be punished. Hindu mythology provides the vocabulary with which to localise and reduce the Western mythologies that, in permitted ignorance of other cultural systems, mistake their local stories for the narrative of world truth. Hanging in one of the figure's hands is a photocopy of another image of an active woman punishing male evil and threat, Artemisia Gentileschi's *Judith and Holofernes* (*c*. 1620). This story itself has a colonial dimension, since the Jewish heroine was appropriated by Christian culture and her meanings so completely refigured that it is still difficult to define what the popularity of this imagery meant at the time a seventeenth-century woman painter began a series of repeated engagements with it.

In Sutapa Biswas's image, the xerox functions as a metonymic sign for Western feminist art history, which celebrates both Gentileschi and her image as *exceptional* because the prevailing notions of femininity as passivity seem to be disrupted in this work by the creation of a murderous heroine. Set in diminished proportions against Indian culture's major deity, Kali, this 'femininity' is made relative while the powerful image from Hindu culture functions to displace stereotypes of Asian women's passivity.

It also reveals complexity and contradiction in Indian culture itself. Gayatri Chakravorty Spivak, in her essay 'Imperialism and Sexual Difference', argues that feminism functions to expose the truth claims of the discourse of the privileged male of the white race, but that often this same feminism fails to acknowledge its own complicity in imperialist discourse. This is revealed particularly in (Western) feminism's ascription, to Western women writers, of a kind of full and therefore ambivalent subjectivity, while either ignoring African, Asian and Arab women or constituting them as a homogeneous collectivity, Third World Women.[01] Sutapa Biswas's Kali-as-housewife uses an image from Hindu culture precisely to overwhelm that objectification, without rewriting her in the mode of bourgeois individualism.

This work was produced in tandem with a remarkable performance, recorded and exhibited as a video. At the time, I had felt privileged and trusted to be invited to witness, so I thought, a performance Sutapa Biswas was preparing in order to explore her double vision.[02] Her feminism was, in a sense, literally larger, broader and more finely calibrated to the questions of difference and power than that within which I had been allowed ignorantly to remain. When

I arrived to watch, I was inexplicably kept waiting in the corridor while preparations continued inside the room. At last I was ushered in to find myself not a spectator at the margins, but part of the spectacle. The centre, British imperialism, was to be put on display and made to figure as part of the rituals of a contestation of its hegemony. Obliged to sit in the centre of a circle, hooded, though I could just see through the slits at eye level, I was made to function as an icon of imperialism around which Biswas's enactments of resistance would be performed. Centred, yet made vulnerable by being deprived of the position of protected observer, I could not distance myself from the mythological representation of a historically conditioned struggle, which was concretised in Sutapa Biswas's experience as an Asian student in a British university art department. The processes by which colonialism happens 'elsewhere', over there and not at home, and the temporal devices by which colonised peoples are displaced backwards in time as if they belonged to a past, or a timeless zone, statically captured by religions and cultures that are ethnographically recorded as being stuck in the time immemorial when they began, were thwarted in this work by the proximity of real persons in a space that performance

Pied Piper of Hamlyn – Put Your Money Where Your Mouth Is, 1987. Acrylics, pastel, pencil and colour xerox collage on paper. 206 x 151.8cm each. Collection Arts Council of England.

26

rewrote as the space of history and power and resistance.

Participant yet target, forced to hear and struggle to see meanings that silenced me, I was made witness to the making of another set of subjectivities, which exploded the oppositions – black/white, Indian/English – in order to demand mutual recognition based on the mutuality or interdependency of subjectivities and meanings. Imperialism functions in its colonial as well as classed and gendered forms as the privilege of neutrality. The imperial subject is made to feel itself the norm, without colour, sex, difference. The difference and its injuries are projected out, to be carried and signified by that which is othered in terms of class, race, gender, ability and so forth. Purely positive endorsement of the other's *otherness* – any form of essentialist and uncritical celebration of ethnicity, class, culture, femaleness – may offer momentary solidarity and necessary affirmation, but it nonetheless confirms the mythic structure of the opposition, leaving it in place while reversing the evaluation of its terms. People who are the products of imperialism cannot sustain this binary opposition and its use of distance, for we carry the imbrication of world cultures within us. Whiteness, Europeanness,

maleness and so forth depend for their meanings on that which they 'other', even while they use the *othered* to exnominate, to disguise themselves. In the movements of peoples and the circulation of goods and cultures, there are no more discrete cultures and radically fixed differences. Some see the present situation as a kind of postmodern hybridity, others stress the ambivalence that underlies our inevitable complexity as postcolonial subjects, and Sutapa Biswas's work operates in these mutually contaminated spaces through which she can explore this historically specific subjectivity.

Since that performance, she has travelled literally and metaphorically to other spaces, and her work now retains the imprint of this concern with space and the positioning of the viewer in relation to an experience of the work that is not contained by sight. Standard spectatorship allows the viewer, first, a distance from the object, and, second, renders what is seen an object, objectifying in turn the subject who has produced the work. Sutapa Biswas seeks ways to undermine this metaphorically imperialist spectatorship. Initially this interest revealed itself in the way she used the spaces of the two-dimensional surfaces of drawings and pastels. Scale is important;

to be confronted with very large pictures alters the spectator's own sense of importance in relation to the figured presences of the images. But Biswas also uses the blank, unworked spaces of the paper. These read in several ways.

On the one hand, they imply a sophisticated engagement with the problematics of modernism, which specified the particularity of painting as the flatness of the support, in opposition to the illusion of three-dimensionality achieved by the use of perspective devices. Biswas's figures elaborate that flatness while yet stressing it. Pastel is used to indicate the rounded forms of well-muscled arms, yet its own materiality insistently draws attention to its placing on the surface. Areas of dense colour, which always threaten to advance or recede, are held in check by the overall pattern shaped both like an eye and a mouth, which, for instance, appears on the garments of Kali and the figures in *As I Stood, Listened and Watched, My Feelings Were This Woman Is Not For Burning* (Part I, 1985). Such devices, which so affirmatively define the surface of the paper on which she works, yield yet another semantic dimension. Modernism here serves feminist concerns in refusing the eye the fascinations of the female body – so adamantly not on offer precisely because of the density of the skin of colour, which in modernist practice stands in as signifier for the body that masculine fantasy nonetheless desires to see.

On the other hand, the empty surfaces also engage with modernist concerns critically rather than sycophantically. Sutapa Biswas refers to the impact of Robert Rauschenberg's series of *White Paintings* (1951) encountered perhaps in Fred Orton's lecture course on American culture and society in the 1950s. Entirely blank canvases, ironically the epitome of modernism's purity, these nonetheless were full of incident, caused by their interaction with an environment and the spectator, whose own presence is traced on the pristine surface. Sutapa Biswas used this insight in her own work quite differently at first. Large areas of unworked surface create not a blank space of nothing, but a counterpoint to what is so energetically worked. Using modernist notions of flatness and surface, she can make the figured and the as-yet unmarked, the full and the seemingly empty, work in tension, a creative incongruity that makes the viewer recognise that what seems empty may still signify, may still be active in contributing to the impact and meaning of the whole. This notion of other space,

28

space off, brought into play, continues to be explored in a variety of practices that ultimately lead Biswas back towards the spaces of interaction so specific to performance, without abandoning the spaces of representation, or indeed represented space.

Sutapa Biswas has described the impact on her work of a journey to India in 1987, her first in twenty-one years, a journey that both involved a going back to the times and spaces of a remembered childhood and to the times and spaces of a historical India, one of the cultural compass points that she had been working from to negotiate her specific position within contemporary British culture. She visited the cave temples of Ajanta and Ellora, the temples of Orissa and Khajuraha, and records the significance of the encounters with these architectural realisations on her interest in the interactions of individuals with physical space, which lead away from the fetishising spectatorship typical of Western art to the multilayered semiotic experience characteristic of ritual or ceremonial architecture, with its varied uses of sculpture and painted imageries within a spatial totality that acts upon the participant.

These discoveries did not serve merely formal purposes, for the relation of Sutapa Biswas herself to these places was not merely antiquarian or scholarly. She came to them not only through space, from England back to India, but through time, from professional art practice in adulthood to childhood memory and family. What the discoveries in India offered, and why these places meant so much, is determined within a specific subject's configuration of a widespread contemporary condition of displacement, memory, and desire. Indeed, this condition may be one of the decisive formations of postmodern subjectivity, which those writers and artists who do not merely straddle two cultures, but embody the pain and pleasures of a historically shaped multiplicity, are now finding forms to signify.

That this is a post- or anti-Orientalist programme cannot be doubted. It is significant that Sutapa Biswas's historical studies at Leeds involved a critique of what Edward Said called 'Orientalism' in Western painting, particularly of the nineteenth century.[03] Orientalism refers to the array of political, scholarly and aesthetic discourses that turned a Western gaze upon the Islamic world and invented an 'Orient', an 'East', as the cipher of difference by which a European selfhood and identity was constructed as both superior and dominant. Orientalism as a form of domination was constructed by a variety of strategies and devices; it is a projection of both fear and fascination whose interactions create its characteristic myths of Oriental backwardness, laziness, sensuality, cruelty, luxury and indifference. Orientalism furthermore creates a temporal ellipsis, which projects that which is named as the Orient as belonging to a permanent past; the European colonial invasion is then represented as merely the inevitable rescue of dying cultures, which will be brought into the present by becoming subjected to a Europe thus made synonymous with modernity. Domination then reads as progress. Orientalism is, in the words of Gayatri Chakravorty Spivak, a process of 'worlding', for the actual interventions of the European colonisers as soldiers, traders, scholars, artists and governors involved a process of moving from ignorance of societies and cultures that were illegible to them, treating India as a kind of uninscribed earth, towards their own mapping, the imposition of their own schemes of meaning through which the colonised were then invited to recognise themselves. This metaphor of cartography – which marks the blank inert earth with the colonisers' meaning, thus making it a world, yielding meanings for its subjects – she calls the 'epistemic violence of the imperialist project'.[04] It once again involves notions of space, a semiotics of space, which has to be engaged with and rewritten, reworlded by the artist who wishes to explore the ambivalence and multivalence of that history, avoiding the mythologising of East, Orient and otherness, which, by virtue of evacuating history, remains in the imaginary spaces of Orientalism and imperialism.

Sutapa Biswas has written of her project as attempting to 'demythologise' otherness. This term also evokes the critical work of Roland Barthes, whose study of 'Myth Today' was written at the height of France's Orientalist crisis, the Algerian struggles in the late 1950s for liberation from France's colonial domination. He used as his example of myth as the prevailing semiotic form of bourgeois representation the front cover of *Paris Match*, which showed an African soldier saluting the French tricolour. Myth is what Barthes calls a depoliticised form of speech. It works by appropriating one level of meaning, such as that which results from our decoding the colour photograph as the picture of an African man in a French uniform saluting a French flag, and then emptying these fully constituted signs of their historical specificity so that they can be filled up

30

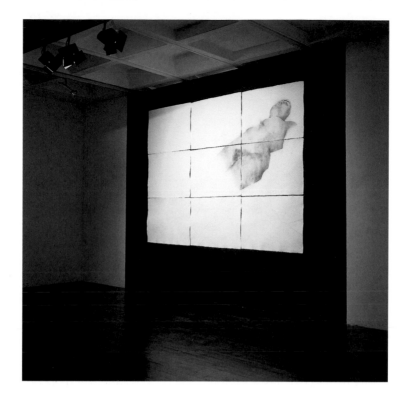

To Touch Stone, 1991. Line drawing on cotton rag paper. 180 x 240cm. Arnolfini Gallery, Bristol, UK. Photograph: Eddie Chambers.

with a more dispersed, yet globalising, meaning: French imperiality. Barthes uses a number of terms to describe this complex process of the ideological colonisation of signs. Myth appropriates, making the first level of meaning the accomplice of the mythic sense. Myth deforms, distances, distorts. But it never completely obliterates:

> [W]hat French imperiality obscures is also a primary language, a factual discourse which was telling me about the salute of the African in uniform. But this distortion is not an obliteration: the… African remains here, the concept needs them; they are half amputated, they are deprived of memory, not of existence; they are at once stubborn, silently rooted there, and garrulous, a speech wholly at the service of the concept. The concept, literally, deforms, but does not abolish the meaning; a word can perfectly render this contradiction: it alienates it.[05]

Alienate has several meanings. It is about rendering something alien, making it other and foreign. It also means separating what belongs to someone from them, in the sense of alienating affections, or property, or, in Marxist terms, the rights to the product of a person's own labour. In psychological parlance, it refers to the subjective experience of not feeling at one with oneself, or feeling cut off from those with whom we should or would like to feel close. *Alienate* is a promiscuous and labile word, but it nonetheless captures the condition of the imperialised subject – made other, thus cut off from its own centre and made to feel separate from what should be close, affirmative, comfortable, and also deprived of the products of culture and labour, which are represented as cut off, unavailable for use in the present. To demythologise is thus to undermine and resist that alienation, that being made to feel alien in one's own land, time, family and person.[06] The myth produced by imperialism/Orientalism is that there are other lands, rather than the spaces of interaction. To contest that myth is to refuse to be constructed as 'belonging elsewhere'. For Asian artists born in India and growing up in Britain, for those intellectuals who actively see themselves living across the mythic spaces of a postcolonial world, through the accidents of birth and professional work or through growing up in the West as part of an Asian culture, refusing in their persons

31

to confirm that division, the critical project is the articulation of this demythologised, de-alienated space. Its articulation can be achieved precisely in the spaces of representation, 'fabled territories', as the title of a currently touring exhibition of new Asian photography in Britain names it.

Photography is a specifically cogent form of representation within which to work this problematic through. Sutapa Biswas has used it in her *Infestations of the Aorta – Shrine to a Distant Relative* (1989) and other works. Photographic space simultaneously contains fact and fantasy. It can make images concrete because we are led to believe what we are shown photographically. Yet it has always been a fantastic medium, for it stays time, freezing the moment into a perpetual past that can be held and looked at in the present. It can record, yet also be the means of representing entirely fabricated scenarios that access memory and feed desire. Barthes defines myth as depriving the image of memory while appropriating its existence. Sutapa Biswas's work demythologises by activating memory precisely. In a literal, autobiographical sense, she makes use of the memories that she reactivated on her trip to India to revisit the places associated with her childhood

(see *Blue Skies and Sunday Lunch*, 1989). But, as well, her installations aim to create the space of memory that is also historical and cultural. The personal can become a mythic signifier because it can be used to absent the historical context in which we are produced as subjects. The othered, colonised subject is alienated from history and memory, made into a static fetish of its exoticism. To insist upon subjectivity, through play of memory and desire, is to return time, history and society as the context of our experience.

How can that be managed in an art practice? Sutapa Biswas orchestrates the space of her exhibition so that she is the author of an entire installation. This was most marked in the piece/event/installation *Sacred Space* (1990). She used a room in the Slade School of Art, London University, a neighbour of the School of Oriental and African Studies established in 1909, and forced into view the architecture of Orientalism. Said quotes arch-Orientalist politician Lord Cromer, advocating in the British Parliament the foundation of this school: 'The creation of a school [of Oriental studies, later to become the London University School of Oriental and African Studies] like this in London is *part of the*

32

Left: *Sacred Space II*, 1990. Pastel and line drawing on paper, 144 x 111.5cm.

Right: *Sacred Space I, II* and *III*, 1990. Pastel, acrylics and line drawing on paper. Installation view, Slade School of Art, University College, London.

furniture of Empire.'[07] She carefully restored the room so that its pristine whiteness marked the division between its space and that of the decaying building. The lights installed outside the windows caused the room itself to become one vast 'white painting' constantly reworked by the play of natural and artificial light in ways that Sutapa Biswas affirms were suggested by the paintings of rooms by American painter Edward Hopper. Mounted on the walls behind nonreflective glass were three large, framed images: pastel, line drawing and acrylic. Again these images were placed on large white surfaces whose edges were hard to discern against the surrounding whiteness of the walls. The subtle erosion of the boundaries between picture and space almost suggested that the images were drawn directly on the walls, and the viewer was thus incited to move in for closer inspection. At that distance the hanging of the piece and its size emphasised an architectural space, in which the viewer cannot imagine him/herself merely the mastering eye, but knows him/herself as a body in space.

On another wall was mounted, at a top eye level of 1.8 metres, a series of black-and-white photographic images. Printed onto litho film and mounted as transparencies pressed between glass, they were further textured by the wall behind. Yet they were framed, holding the flow of spaces, so that the viewer – coming close to read the texts and the images, which were constantly being eroded by light reflecting on them from outside – had to work to see and read. Participant, engaged, worked on, the viewer becomes visitor to the installation, which put Sutapa Biswas's world, that which she as artist has 'worlded'[08] and thus inscribed with her meanings, into a special kind of encounter with that visitor. Like my own experience as decentred witness to her early performance, the work is experienced as both invitation, drawing us closer and making us do bodily work to read the signs, and challenge, because the work so insistently embodies the subjectivity of the artist who made this space 'sacred'.

Of memory, we change
From one conversation to the next
Always in search of
The edge of the surface
And of textures
There is pleasure
and sometimes none

So thinking back to our space
Marked only by fallen clay
There is both absence and presence

Of violated territories –

You, whose spirit is dull
Brought me here
To the great mountain
Whereupon, I died in the thinness of its air
From violated territories
Its boundaries,
With fierce eyes
I watch
This sacred space.
Sutapa Biswas, 1990

The images in the photographs are those of a bare foot stepping in footsteps imprinted in the sand. For some this will conjure up both Freud's reflections on Jensen's *Gradiva* [09] and Victor Burgin's photo-work of the same title, which reflects on Freud's essay, using the fetish of the beautiful and lost girl's unsandalled foot glimpsed at Pompeii. Such formal parallels serve to give this work its sense of belonging here and now to a world that includes both Freud and a critical semiotic art practice that invokes psychoanalysis precisely to insist upon questions of subjectivity in the production and consumption of art. Complexities of desire, not nostalgia for some lost homeland, are the animating terms of Sutapa Biswas's use of memory, image and space. Psychoanalysis argues that in our formation as human subjects we become human only as we are marked by loss and lack, which results in the specific configuration of our subjectivity as split, conscious/unconscious, each of which has its own characteristic modes of meaning. But between both there is a perpetual if displaced traffic, by means of which the journeys we undertook to become subjects can be viewed as an archaeological site: every stage is sedimented within us, but its form's survival is affected by all other stages and their related traumas. The multilayered spaces of the subject can be evoked and addressed in the multilayered spaces of the installation, where image, surface, space, figure, body and sign are put into orchestrated tension and play.

The body in space functions as a literal sign of real subjects in a concrete history, which is the territory

As I Stood, Listened and Watched, My Feelings Were This Woman Is Not for Burning, 1985. Diptych. Pastel and acrylics on paper. 183 x 91cm. Collection of Bradford City Museums and Art Galleries, Cartwright Hall, UK.

on which we must engage in dialogue about the epistemic violence of imperialism and the violated territories of its subjects. That acknowledgment is neither comfortable nor painless for any of those caught in its historic webs. But there is no other space, utopic or nostalgic, that will heal the rifts in our persons, as human subjects, in our social beings, as products of a real history. There is no essential Mother India to salve the wounds of displacement and separation, but, in Sutapa Biswas's work, there is a confrontation with the loss of and grief for an actual grandmother who was the beloved figure of childhood. There is no universal space called 'art' or 'being human' that can relieve the pain caused by learning about whiteness and Western power; but by attending to the articulation of the specificity of someone's experience, that person can then be seen as not 'other' but particular, distinct from yet shaped by whiteness and its West.

In her aesthetic fashioning of the spaces of contiguity for India and Britain these are made contemporaries, and while the interaction of the two is particular to Sutapa Biswas (precisely because she makes their imbrication the condition of her practice), they become part of the viewer's world too.

The body in space thus functions as an allegory for the problems and disjunctions of communication, connection and disconnection, hearing and distortion, projection and confrontation. Who is made present by participating in Sutapa Biswas's work is the subject of history.

But even as I write this I realise that it once again inscribes a Western worlding. There is no subject, but always subjects; there is no history, but always histories. I have so far stressed the issues of imperialism, its subjectivities and histories, because it is the condition of Sutapa Biswas's work. In our conversations at Leeds, it was the legacy of racism that rendered my feminism both local and imperial. Feminism is not displaced by the politics of race; just as there has always been black women's creativity, there has also always been black feminism. Yet to qualify women's creativity and feminism with a signifier of colour is to become enmeshed with the ideological constructions of racism. Sutapa Biswas's feminism challenged the ideological limits of what Valerie Amos and Pratibha Parmar named 'Imperial Feminism'.[10] They quote bell hooks' argument about the racism inside the women's movement: that feminist scholarship is written as if black women were not a part of the collective group of women.[11] Thus, a feminism that perpetuates its own ethnocentricity actively perpetuates racism. Amos and Parmar critically examine some of the key theoretical concepts of white feminist literature to examine their pertinence for black feminist theory. Difference, family and sexuality are all qualified by being examined in relation to the specificity of the experiences of Asian women and women of African descent. There is an important link here with *Housewives with Steak-Knives*, which is also a powerful text about femininity: Western ideologies of both Western and Asian femininity (which is associated with passivity) are interrupted and set in tension both by the fact of Biswas's active creativity and her use of an image of female power, Kali. Writing of Sutapa Biswas's work in the context of the politics of modernism and postmodernism, Gilane Tawadros calls this painting the 'clearest enunciation of… black femininity as a form of creative resistance':[12]

Here, Hindu mythology is invoked to serve a political content which is quintessentially modern. The image of the goddess, Kali…

has been appropriated by Biswas as a means of dissolving the absolute distinction and binary oppositions which characterise European thought. In opposition to these false and essentialist categories, the precepts of Hindu culture reflect the ascendancy of ambivalence. Thus, the Western notion of 'femininity' as essentially fragile and passive is contested by the ambivalent status of… Kali who is at once both the goddess of war and peace. In adapting the Hindu iconography of Kali, then, Biswas asserts the ambivalence of femininity, both pacifist (as opposed to passive) and aggressive, both 'feminine' in a traditional sense and strong. She also affirms the existence, in terms of the Hindu system of knowledge, of a 'zone of indiscernibility' to borrow Gilles Deleuze's phrase, between myth and reality. Thus, Biswas, implies, there is an element of the real in the mythologisation of 'femininity' and, equally, an element of myth in the reality of black womanhood.[13]

Tawadros also suggests that by using icons and myths (from Indian and Western art and culture)

The Only Good Indian…, 1985.
Mixed media on paper, 200 x 193cm.
Leicester City Council Collection.

Sutapa Biswas suggests a fusion between past and present, a way in which history is activated for the present, while also acknowledging other temporalities embodied in myth and religious thought. Finally, she points out the corruption of the key Western distinction between public and private, which is a gendering of social as well as psychic space, associating the feminine with the domestic and the private in opposition to the supposedly masculine domains of politics, power and action. In this work, and later drawings from the same period, the housewife and her domestic tools, knife here, potato peeler in *The Only Good Indian*… (1985), become tools of aggressive defiance because domestic spaces are perceived as penetrated by the politics of gender and of race power, which is equally the site of resistance. Indeed, the family space is a critical one for Asian women in the struggle with white and black patriarchs, with the imperial state and its racist immigration and employment policies. The complexity of the mutually inflected struggles requires the production of artworks that are not ambivalent in a typically postmodern avoidance of accountability, politics and ethics, but which are *cogently* ambivalent in order to invent multiple

registers of meaning, activated in the spatial encounter between subjects with bodies and histories, and the cultural inscriptions of a British Asian woman artist.

Not so much beyond the boundary as a perpetual crossing, eroding and unfixing of the frontiers where we must engage in dialogue, self-recognition and acknowledgment of difference within the realisation of complexity and ambivalence. Through the use of many media, formats and installations in space, Sutapa Biswas orchestrates a highly *affective* aesthetic staging for a non-hierarchical 'worlding' – where desire, fascination, pleasure and pain are inscribed and evoked. Footprints in the sand are fragile and transitory, yet their pressure leaves the trace of an other's journey or pathway, which we are invited to follow. Sutapa Biswas's materials increasingly invoke the notion of the trace, the fragile imprint in the historical and cultural archive of people's bodies, memories and experiences. If we can all invest these traces with the full though not undivided subjectivity that they signify, we can begin to resist the alienation of mythology (in Barthes's sense, the making foreign, the depriving of what is of or belongs to oneself), and in particular the West's destructive use of foreignness and its fear of ambivalence.[14] The binary oppositions of Western culture – white/black, self/other, here/there, man/woman, to name but a few – are very local yet destructively hegemonic. Positioning her work as a historical practice, dialectical, full of interaction and mutual determination, while fashioning its poetics at the level of the intimate, tactile, personally charged, Sutapa Biswas produces a powerful, empowering and critically feminist text that enlarges the world by overlaying and thus mutually redefining these oppositions, of which yet one more is that of centre and periphery. Gilane Tawadros states:

> The constellation of voices and the plurality of meanings which are postulated by postmodernity serve to obscure its continuities with cultural modernism and suggests, perhaps, that this may not be a fissure or 'new dawn' in European consciousness but merely a transformation of the grand narratives of the West. In this context, the 'populist modernism' of black cultural practice, I would argue, signals a critical reappropriation of modernity which stems from an assertion of history and historical processes. Black women's creativity in particular expresses the ambivalence of identity and redundancy of exclusive and unambiguous absolutes. It dissolves the fixed boundaries between past and present, public and private, personal and political.[15]

According to Tawadros, '[T]he cultural expression of the margins and the periphery represents an aesthetic and political project'; the cultural practice of Sutapa Biswas, she argues, is the space of the diaspora, a space that is predicated not on the primacy of difference and dispersion, but on 'resistance and change'.[16]

Edited version first published in *Synapse: New Photographic Work by Sutapa Biswas*, exhibition catalogue, London and Leeds: The Photographers' Gallery and Leeds City Art Galleries, 1992.

Notes

01_Gayatri Chakravorty Spivak, 'Imperialism and Sexual Difference', *Oxford Literary Review*, 1986, no. 8, pp. 225–40.
02_The phrase derives from the work of the American feminist historian Joan Kelly, 'The Doubled Vision of Feminist Theory' (1979), in Joan Kelly, *Women, History and Theory*, Chicago: University of Chicago, 1984. Kelly identifies a double vision as that which embraces both the private and public spheres of Western bourgeois society. I am using it here for Sutapa Biswas's project, which creates two centres in conflict and dialogue, each having to acknowledge that the other is always-already a part of the other, because they are both lived by the subjects – women subjects, colonial subjects. (This last phrase implies both coloniser and colonised and in doing so acknowledges the colonised as also a subject of the process, and not merely the passive object of Europe's othering.)
03_Edward Said, *Orientalism*, London: Routledge and Kegan Paul, 1978.
04_Gayatri Chakravorty Spivak, 'The Rani of Sirmur: An Essay in Reading the Archives', *History and Theory*, 1985, vol. 8, p. 251.

05_Roland Barthes, 'Myth Today', in *Mythologies* (1957), trans. Annette Lavers, London: Paladin, 1973, pp. 122–23.
06_This idea is powerfully explored in Frantz Fanon, *Black Skin, White Masks* (1952), London: Pluto Press, 1986.
07_Said, op. cit., p. 213.
08_Spivak derives her concept from the philosopher Heidegger, who used it to define the origins of the work of art as resulting from the gap between earth and world, a gap filled by the texture and substance of the artwork.
09_Sigmund Freud, 'Delusions and Dreams in Jensen's *Gradiva*' (1907), in Freud, *On Art & Literature*, Pelican Freud Library, vol. 14, London: Pelican Books, 1985.
10_Valerie Amos and Pratibha Parmar, 'Challenging Imperial Feminism', *Feminist Review*, 1984, no. 17, pp. 3–20.
11_bell hooks, *Ain't I a Woman: Black Women and Feminism*, London: Pluto Press, 1982.
12_Gilane Tawadros, 'Beyond the Boundary: The Work of Three Black Women Artists in Britain', *Third Text*, 1989, issue 8/9, p. 145.
13_Ibid.

14_Both themes have just been treated by two important Western thinkers, Zygmunt Bauman (*Modernity and Ambivalence*, Cambridge: Polity Press, 1991) and Julia Kristeva (*Strangers to Ourselves*, trans. Leon Roudiez, Brighton: Harvester Wheatsheaf Press, 1991).
15_Tawadros, op. cit., p. 150.
16_Ibid.

Spaces Inside Time
Guy Brett

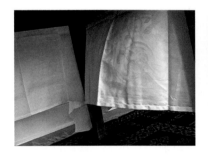

Untitled, 2003. Video still.

Recently, Sutapa Biswas has produced a number of scenarios in which time almost stands still. The video *The Trials and Tribulations of Mickey Baker* (1997) presents us with the side view of a portly late middle-aged man, naked, standing in a furnished room. He rocks slightly on his feet as he breathes and leaves stir in the sunlight outside the window; there is little other movement as the tape loops and begins again. In *Untitled (Bit Part)* (1999–2003), a double video projection, the left-hand screen shows a child of about two crawl-climbing and descending a steep carpeted staircase; on the right-hand screen appears an extract from a bar scene from John Huston's 1961 film *The Misfits*. Both sequences are slowed down considerably.

In a third video we see the underneath of a table with its tablecloth shifting starchily in a light breeze. In a fourth, *Birdsong*, two screens are again installed side by side. In the opening sequence a suspended silver origami model of a horse with wings is seen revolving from a low angle on each screen; in another take the child (actually Sutapa Biswas's son Enzo, now five years old) sits quietly, his face preoccupied with the presence of some thing or being we cannot see. In a short following sequence this 'something'

is revealed to be a horse, standing saddled in the middle of a rather grandly furnished drawing room.

There is an obvious paradox in using a kinetic medium to portray something that is barely moving. In fact the oxymoron 'static movie' is a fruitful nonsense, as oxymorons often are. The phenomenon was famously adopted by Andy Warhol in films like his *Empire* (1964, a seven-hour fixed camera shot of the Empire State Building). In the 'movie' sense time stands still, but in the 'real' sense time is seen passing. Such perceptions are locked into the evolution and conventions of art forms. In the development of European theatre from the sixteenth to the nineteenth century audiences were amazed by the ever-increasing speed and ingenuity of scene changes (the Venetians were great innovators in this respect). The 'cut' in early cinema introduced instantaneous transfer from one place to another, a novel experience it is impossible to recover today. In fact, with the general frenzy of cutting we see in films and television nowadays, a corresponding amazement is often aroused by no cutting, and stillness. In one sense film rediscovers the condition of painting, but there is all the difference in the world between the film of a subject that keeps still and a still

painting or photograph. The difference lies in a way of conveying 'life'.

Sutapa Biswas has spoken of her desire to 'slow time down'. 'How to weigh a sense of time?', she has asked,[01] which could also be expressed as 'how to give time its true weight?' Among her influences, in making films and videos, have been painters who, for her, construct a particular enigma out of a common condition of stillness, Johannes Vermeer, George Stubbs and Edward Hopper for example. So what would be the purpose of slowing time down? It seems to me that slow time in Sutapa Biswas's recent works is a device for awakening memory, gaining a foothold in the flux of time and conveying an insight into human lives.

The underside-of-the-table video hints at the presence of both child and adult in their absence. It is a shot of a part of the adult world dear to the play and imagination of children but never visited by adults. The pairing of the child on the staircase and *The Misfits* footage is a more complex scenario and gives a good deal of latitude for interpretation, although a child/adult dichotomy is very much present. Enzo's exploratory descent and ascent of the stairs is couched in domestic terms but has a stark simplicity

– a ziggurat form – and even mythic overtones. Enzo is a typical child, could stand for all children. *The Misfits*, on the other hand, is a scene of adult mess, a sort of convivial but incoherent meeting of individuals who jostle together without really communicating. This is caught in John Huston's long panning shot around the occupants of the bar. These characters have been described as 'walking wounded… their whole lives written across their faces'.[02] They are not so much the average, the typical, as 'misfits', each an intense subjectivity (and also a famous star or character actor: Marilyn Monroe, Thelma Ritter, Clark Gable, Eli Wallach, etc.) rendered lost and forlorn by the effect of the slow motion.

Amid all the guffaws and lurchings and inane grins (the sort of human condition Goya captured in his late paintings), a child in cowboy gear is lifted up and parked on the bar. In the film Clark Gable and Eli Wallach play latter-day cowboys, who have a horror of becoming wage-earners but are not able to live the life of roaming freedom they dream of. Most of the men keep their cowboy hats on in the bar and hats occupy a large amount of the screen space. It is curious the way the connection with children and horses is carried over into Sutapa Biswas's

subsequent work, *Birdsong*. The horse in *Birdsong* is ostensibly a reference to Stubbs' painting *Lord Holland and Lord Albemarle Shooting at Goodwood* (1759), and to a fantasy voiced by Enzo of stabling a horse in the family living room. But *Birdsong* seems very much a further meditation on childhood, or on the all-absorbing experience the growth of the child may be for the parent. In the close-up shots of Enzo, before we know what is happening in his environment, there is a slight time lapse between the two adjacent screens. A tiny change of expression or movement is momentarily repeated or echoed in our view, a delicate device which has the effect of emphasising his thoughts, his inner world. As Sutapa Biswas has pointed out, these nuances are minutely revealing, and both time- and context-sensitive. If Enzo was only slightly older his presence would be quite different, more 'worldly', more out in the world, and his relationship to the massive being sharing the space with him would also change.

Of course *The Misfits* quote is not Sutapa Biswas's last word on ageing. We notice that the title of the Mickey Baker video refers to his 'trials and tribulations'. There is no visible sign of these.

The words have a gentle ironic charge since the image itself is one of calm and reflection. He seems to carry his ideosyncratic body with the unselfconscious acceptance of any animal or bird.

A word with particular importance for Sutapa Biswas, being the title of one of her series of works and occurring often in her statements, is 'synapse'. In anatomical terms it describes the electro-chemical relationship of one nerve cell to another. For the artist it takes on a broad metaphorical meaning as 'that point of exchange between two or more components… a relationship in which each of us is cited and sited'.[03] *Synapse* was the title of an exhibition she made after a journey to India in 1986–87: a very significant journey of re-encounter with the country in which she was born, but left with her parents at the age of three. Whatever the multitude of sensations and memories the visit may have aroused, the experience was distilled in a series of photographs based on a simple device: the projection of images of the sculpted walls of India's temples on her naked body. If the device is simple, all the nuance and sensibility is in the way the liquid light falls across the body in the surrounding darkness, an intimate, somewhat hesitant dialogue

Untitled (Bit Part), 1999–2003. Video stills. The corresponding right-hand screen to this work shows a scene from *The Misfits*, which the publishers were not granted permission to reproduce.

Marilyn Monroe, Malibu 1948, no. 1.
© Bill Burnside 1948/Marilyn Monroe.
Reproduced by kind permission of the
Estate of Fenton Bresler. This is the
first in a series of four postcards, shot
in the same location, that the artist
acquired in 1990. The discomfort
in Monroe's pose is a source of
inspiration for the precariousness of
the shots shown in *Untitled (Bit Part)*.

of flesh and stone, ancient stone which represents and celebrates the body as a spiritual emblem.

The combination of 'citing and siting' in the process of coming to terms with the experience of being born in one culture (or 'psycho-geographic' reality) and growing up in another leads to the broader definition of synapse. 'Synapse is a place where two people meet. Synapse is a gap across which ideas meet.'[04] Sutapa Biswas has always chosen to interpret this metaphor in a wide and diverse sense. She studied Fine Art at the University of Leeds at the beginning of the 1980s, at a time when the courses were strongly influenced by radical politics: the women's movement, socialism and anti-colonialism. The legacy of the art historian T.J. Clark had been taken up by a generation of teachers that included Griselda Pollock, Terry Atkinson, Fred Orton and John Tagg. Facing a choice for the subject of her dissertation, she wavered between the surrealist painter Leonore Fini and the work of young black and Asian women artists in Britain. She chose the latter and remained strongly identified with that tendency, grouping or movement, appearing in such exhibitions as *The Thin Black Line* (ICA, London, 1985), *The Essential Black Art* (Chisenhale Gallery, London,

1988) and *The Unmapped Body: 3 Black British Artists* (Yale University Art Gallery, Connecticut, 1998) (both of the latter two shows included male artists). At the same time she was drawn to the happenings of Claes Oldenburg and Robert Rauschenberg, Rauschenberg's *White Paintings* (1951), and John Cage's music and philosophy. The meeting, or reciprocal interaction of ideas, was what most interested her. 'I sought to find a language that deliberately brought together components that were both of a Western and an Eastern aesthetic and ideology. For me, the phenomenon didn't present such distinct borders, but in fact there were similarities and parallels in both camps.'[05]

This leads us to the somewhat intricate role the synapse is playing in her newest work. One manifestation that can continue to be followed is in terms of the child/adult dichotomy, or meeting. It appears again in *Magnesium Bird* (2004), a work still in progress at the time of writing this essay, whose details may well change. In a film to be shot in the eighteenth-century walled garden of Harewood House near Leeds, small kids will play among the trees at the far end of the orchard in front of the greenhouses. Originally, the film was to be shot in

The Orange=colour Bird.

The Yellow Bird.

The Dark Blue Bird.

The Lilac Bird.

Left: The artist's set of four less comic birds, 2004. Watercolour and pencil on paper, 20.5 x 14.8cm.

Above: Edward Lear, *Set of Four Comic Birds*, c. 1880. Pen and ink and watercolour, 14 x 11cm. © V&A Images.

Notes
01__Sutapa Biswas, 'To Kill Two Birds with One Stone', in *Locus+ 1993–1996*, edited by Samantha Wilkinson, Newcastle-upon–Tyne: Locus+, 1996, p. 37.
02__*The Misfits*, review by Damian Cannon, www.film.u-net.com.
03__Sutapa Biswas: *Synapse*, limited edition artist's book, Vancouver, 1991.
04__Sutapa Biswas, 'To Kill Two Birds with One Stone', *Camerawork: A Journal of Photographic Arts*, vol. 23, no. 2, Fall/Winter 1996, p. 30.
05__Sutapa Biswas and Moira Roth, 'Sutapa Biswas – A Narrative Chronology', *Synapse*, op. cit., p. 23.

the hothouses of Kew Gardens, with the sound of the children replacing the singing birds and crickets which are strangely absent from an otherwise luxuriant scene. Reference will be made to the fact that birds were the subject of Sutapa Biswas's final conversation with her father, and that the first sound she heard after his death was birdsong. The bird reference will extend to the figure of the nineteenth-century writer and artist Edward Lear, where it will make an imaginative leap to connect again with the adult/child theme. Edward Lear represents a fascinating complexity, not only of Victorian intellect and culture but of human consciousness in general. On the one hand Lear possessed the serious, scientific, adult mindset of the ornithologist. (Lear made exquisitely precise drawings of parrots in Lord Derby's menagerie and aviary at Knowsley Hall, on Merseyside. We read that he insisted on drawing from living birds rather than, as was customary then, from stuffed skins.) On the other hand, he had the imaginative, poetic, playful mind of the fantasist who produced what Lear himself called Nonsense and could only address to children. A 'scientific' and a 'nonsense' bird drawn by Edward Lear can be placed side by side, can 'meet'.

When that happens the effect is deeply revealing: two kinds of truth shine out, coexisting in the same person, one no less real than the other. The reference to Edward Lear weaves in a further working of the synapse analogy: in this case a mind where two minds meet.

Birdsong
Laura Mulvey

The cinema is essentially a medium of temporal duration. But within this duration, depiction of time may vary. Usually, the cinema's depiction of time is tied to the illusion of movement. The appearance and aesthetic of natural movement, and its extraordinary ability to mimic human perception of human life, has made the cinema into the great storyteller and recorder that it is. Of course, as everyone knows, this mimicking, this aesthetic of natural movement, is an illusion that is achieved by filming and projecting a series of still images, the film strip, at approximately twenty-four frames per second. But the history of cinema, almost from its very beginning, has also seen explorations of a complex temporality that the mass of, mainly narrative, films has tended to conceal. In the first instance, there is a basic contradiction between the cinema's movement and the still frame of the celluloid strip. Stillness and movement: while the moving image echoes human perception of the world, stillness echoes the frozen image to which human production of art (including photography) has been tied for so long. One has the familiarity of nature, the other the familiarity of culture. However, in between these extremes are a range of other temporalities that have little or no connection with human perception of time or its realisation in naturalised movement, for instance, repetition, reversal, stretching time by slowing the image, extending duration. With devices like these, the iconic element, the content, in a specific image may begin to recede and be replaced by the heavy weight of temporality itself materialised in all its uncertainty. And this effect may, in turn, generate a glimmering awareness that human consciousness creates pattern and order to avoid the unspeakable and intractable nature of time itself, of its passing and, ultimately, of death.

Time has always been a significant theme in Sutapa Biswas's work. But in her new installation, *Birdsong* (2004), time has become a more explicit theme and she uses the formal attributes of the moving image to evoke questions about the relation between temporalities and human imagination. Form and content not only alternate in visibility but one also enhances the other, so that the moving image's own temporal attributes lead to themes and motifs about time and its representation and then back again. This is a piece of great thematic richness. It is organised into four shots, each of which is shown doubled, placed next to one another inside a black screen. The piece opens and closes with a shot of a little winged horse, exquisitely made from folded paper, that hangs from a string and rotates on its axis in front of a blurred window frame, in extreme close-up. These two shots of the paper horse 'book-end' the other two shots. In the first, a small boy is shown, in close-up, sitting on a sofa, with a well-furnished sitting room visible in the background. After some time, a large, shadowy presence looms over him, which, with a flick of its tail, reveals itself to be a real live horse. In the second, a long shot shows the horse, standing alone, next to a pool of sunlight that spills on to the floor from the large windows. I want to discuss each shot in turn and then consider the place of time and space also in some of Biswas's previous installations.

The first shot establishes a framework for the representation of time, the key theme throughout the whole piece. In the first instance, the paper horse's movement appears to be seamless as it rotates, creating an effect of timelessness. It does not seem to be a segment of a defined action, something set in motion that will in due course return to stillness. But, as the image persists and as an effect of the duration of the shot itself, the presence of the actual passing of time itself begins to come into play. Theorists of avant-garde film have often pointed out that, conventionally,

a shot is cut according to the length of time needed to absorb its content. Once its duration is pushed further, the spectator can then be brought to consider other key aesthetic elements in its construction. In the case of *Birdsong*, the image begins to suggest the inexorable nature of time's passing, indifferent to human desire or modification and outside cultural or human order. But it is at this point of concentration, at least in my experience, that two further factors come into play. First of all, as the paper horse rotates on its axis, a beam of light catches its body twice as it passes with a silver glow. This moment of highlighting creates the illusion of a slight halt or pause in the seamlessness of the movement that brings a fractional fragmentation to the forward drive of time passing. Secondly, the movement in the separate frames is very slightly out of synch, so that the interaction between the two images of (the same) horse sets in motion another kind of rhythm.

The beam of light first catches one horse as it rotates and then it catches the other, creating a sense of sequence and separation between the two. The images are, however, one and the same. The passing light beam draws attention to the 'now' of an original moment at which the horse's movement had been

Birdsong, 2004.
16mm film, 7mins 7 secs.

registered on celluloid, inscribed by the impact of light itself. A photograph preserves the 'now' of its original moment of registration suspended in time which then, as time passes, evolves into a 'then'. But, as Roland Barthes and other theorists have pointed out, the magical and fascinating quality of the photograph lies in the continued presence of the original 'now' that maintains the coexistence of past and present in one image. It is this aspect of the photograph that defies the logic of time experienced as an inexorable sequence and it produces a temporal conundrum that evades the rules of past, present and future as distinct grammatical forms. It is here that the mechanical nature of photography seems to push towards the edge of a human ability to grasp the nature of time.

In *Birdsong*, this kind of complexity, inherent in the still photograph, is taken further as film, a medium of duration, necessarily exists within a system of series and sequences. As the two, identical images are slightly out of synchronisation, the original moment of the photographic 'now ' is doubled so that impact of the light beam on one horse seems slightly ahead of the other. On close inspection, they appear to move in sequence. The original moment of registration, its preservation in time, is both doubled and ordered

by the moving, as opposed to the still, image. On the one hand, the beauty of the effect stems directly from the non-human nature of film, its mechanical production and reproduction. On the other hand, the illusion of temporal order or sequence owes everything to culture and to the rhythm, or beat, that the two images generate between them. Just as events in narrative film impose their own fictional time on top of the presence of the past, so, in *Birdsong*, the doubling of the image creates a beauty that belongs to the human imagination. Ultimately, the image becomes a vehicle for fantasy and reverie. As the light slows the horse's movement, the temporal pause seems to mutate into a spatial promise. An apparent pause in the continuous movement of time suggests the permeability of surface and the power of the imagination literally to travel through space.

The winged horse is extraordinarily evocative in its own right. It not only evokes the winged horse of Greek mythology, Pegasus, but also that other mythic means of transport, the magic carpet. Both are associated with the kind of travel and adventure that was rarely available to people in ancient times, and with stories and flights of fantasy with which travel is rarely associated now. The paper horse is beautifully folded into the shape of flight and the rhythm set up by the recurring beam of light seems to add a beat to his wings. This is an image that belongs to the storehouse of the human imagination but it is also, in its own right, an object of reverie. From this perspective, it is a figure for the power of imagination, that is, for the human mind's own ability to travel huge distances within seconds, to dream and to conjure up the fantastic. There is something about smallness, the miniature, which seems to be particularly suited to triggering dreams or encapsulating desire. This is, of course, partly to do with the experiences of childhood when the miniature is of an appropriate scale to capture a child's imagination. The horse's connotations of flight and travel necessarily lead out of the framework of time into that of space. The slightly asynchronous movement that creates a moment of pause in the smoothness of time blends into another figure that creates a slight opening, a chink or crack, in the smoothness of the paper horse's rotation. Time mutates into space. But this space of passage or transition only really materialises with the surprise of the following shot.

The second shot of *Birdsong* begins with a fade-up from black into a medium close-up of a small boy. The resonance of daydream, desire and the suggestion of childhood reverie that were all associated with the paper horse can then be attached to his figure. Again, the doubled image and its asynchronous timing add a further level of significance to the image of the child and once again it suggests sequence. But here it evokes a relationship between an interior space of desire and its external expression in bodily gesture. The moment of delay between one image and the other marks the gap between thought and action as though the usually invisible connection between the two could be materialised. The repeated expression seems to enhance a sense of anticipation, as though the child's desire builds expectancy into a premonition of something to come. That is, the world of imagination, created by the previous shot, is transformed into an active wish. As the child sits still but continues to look around him, the shot shows enough of his surroundings to suggest a rather formal sitting room. When the horse appears, he immediately introduces magic into the scene. While the human imagination, however vivid, can only conjure up its desires internally, transforming them into images and myths, the materialisation of wish-fulfilment and fantasy has long-standing associations with the

Jean Cocteau, *La Belle et la Bête*, 1946.
Film still. © Comité Jean Cocteau.

cinema, suspended as it is somewhere between magic and reality. Marina Warner traces the connection back to the early days of film history:

> The new, moving, flux of images held out the enthralling possibility of passing beyond the visible to the (normally) invisible, from the real to the supernatural. What is interesting is how often the supernatural was understood to be subjective – produced by the imagination – and how the communication of internal fantasy became one of the central enterprises of the new 'movies'…. Filmmakers utilised the medium in order to pass through the outer forms in order to reproduce fantasy in almost palpable terms. They explored film's unprecedented power to conjure up the inner workings of the mind.[01]

Birdsong draws on and evokes this rich cinematic tradition in which children's stories and folk tales found new life. The horse's literal materialisation into a space, which is not only interior, but also domestic and even bourgeois, introduces an element of incongruity that once again draws attention to the spatial dimension of the imagination. Folk and fairy tales constantly return to the theme of travel, of leaving home and a transition to another world, which may or may not be a magic one. And the horse, especially the winged horse, as suggested in the opening shot, is a frequently recurring figure enabling travel from the natural world to the supernatural. The hero's journey takes him from the familiarity of home, both its comfort and its constraint, into strangeness and adventure.

In *Birdsong's* third shot, the horse stands quietly at the end of the room, next to a French window that leads to the outside and also allows the outside sunlight to pour into the interior space of the room. The poetically productive opposition between interior and exterior also underlines the way that the horse's presence has bridged the gap between imagination and reality. The creature that should belong to the space of the outside has strangely occupied that of the inside just as the figure of fantasy occupies the imagination. On the other hand, the horse offers the opportunity of an escape, a journey into the outside world with its attractions and its dangers. He stands there as an invitation.

For Sutapa Biswas, *La Belle et la Bête* (Jean Cocteau, France, 1946) has been an important point of reference in the construction of *Birdsong*, for its

54

extraordinary evocation of the transition between worlds, from natural to supernatural, also between folk culture and cinema and finally between storytelling and the imagination of childhood. She has described the impact of the film in the following terms:

> When Belle's father walks through the door of the Beast's palace into a darkened space, a series of arms, on the left side of the frame, hold an exquisite display of candelabra. As he moves through the space, the arms move towards the interior, as if in invitation. It is the sheer magic of this moment that I love. Although it is of course the sheer magic of the film itself that I love. Also wonderful in *La Belle et la Bête*, and similar to Edward Lear's poetry, is the introduction to the film which brings to life the idea of the possibility of the impossible. Written in chalk on a simple blackboard are the words: 'Children believe in stories they are told. They have complete faith. They believe that a plucked rose may bring tragic consequences to a family. They believe in the smoking hands of a beast who kills… and in the shame he feels before the maiden who is his guest. They believe in the countless other artless things. It is a little of this artlessness that I ask of you so that the omens may smile upon all…. Let me pronounce four magic words, that veritable open sesame: "Once Upon A Time".'[02]

There is, however, quite another dimension to the scene depicted in *Birdsong*. As the artist's own son is the child whose daydream comes to life, the piece also bears witness to a mother's perspective and a mother's ambivalence towards the passing of time. The horse represents the fulfilment of a child's fantasy and the excitement of its journey, but also the persistent sense of loss felt by a mother, not only as her child begins to dream of a world outside the home, but also as she feels the gradual impact of separation. According to psychoanalytic theory, particularly, that is, Lacanian theory, the bond between mother and child has to give way to the child's ultimate need to break away from this most satisfying of relationships, both emotional and physical. In Lacanian terms, the mother is marginal to culture and stands in opposition to the father who offers entry into language, knowledge and self-sufficiency. This pattern creates an impermeable binary between father and mother, between a

relationship based on language and one based on pre-language, between the world of culture and that of the body.

Birdsong makes two important contributions to modifying this account of the Oedipal moment that feminist psychoanalytic theory has tended to accept as a description of a strict patriarchal culture while also challenging the necessity of its terms. In the first instance, *Birdsong* creates a world that is in transition, that belongs to childhood and the imagination rather than to maturity and the law, that can be of the maternal but is not external to culture. It is located on a kind of threshold, where the logical rules of time and space do not apply, but the rich culture of fantasy and the imagination flourish. Perhaps what gives this world a special appeal is its relegation to the margins of formal or high culture, bringing together the 'primitive' world of childhood and the 'primitive' traditions of folk belief. Both storytelling to children and folk storytelling are associated with an oral, rather than a literary, tradition and, as Angela Carter[03] points out, both are associated with women, from a mother's bedtime story to old wives' tales. A number of feminist writers and artists have looked to this world as a source for

ideas and images that have great emotional and aesthetic significance but are not fully integrated into 'official' culture. From this perspective, the pre- and post-Oedipal phases are not so rigorously divided, and the binary oppositions mutate into a pleasing, intermediate, space of liminality. Work that draws on this kind of culture not only benefits from its very specific aesthetic but can also build up an alternative to the traditions of art that have excluded women. Furthermore, the time and space of motherhood can become the source of creativity and a site for investigation so that the myth of a marginalised state, in which both mother and child are 'outside' language may be eroded by the process of creativity itself.

However, stillness is the predominant mood of the two central shots in *Birdsong*. Not only are the two interior scenes shot with a still camera but the movements within the frame are also quite minimal. There is a sense that the artist is trying to hold back, or at least hold on to, the passing of time that gradually distances the closeness between mother and child. From this perspective, the piece may be understood as a *pietà*, but one that, in all its complexity, comes directly from the feelings of the

Above left: Untitled, 2001.
Pen and ink on paper, 14.7 x 10.2cm.

Above right: Louise Bourgeois, *I UNDO* (interior detail), 1999–2000.
Steel, stainless steel, wood, glass and epoxy, 1300.4 x 450.2 x 350.5cm.
Courtesy Cheim & Read, New York.
Photograph: Marcus Leith.

Notes
01__Marina Warner, *Cinema and the Realm of Enchantment*, London: British Film Institute, 1993, pp. 14 and 16.
02__Conversation with the artist, January 2004.
03__Angela Carter (ed.), *The Virago Book of Fairy Tales*, London: Virago, 1991, introduction, p. x.

mother rather than one that represents such feelings as eternal, immutable and inaccessible to self-expression. The painterly quality of the images, the rich colours, the sunlight and the composition of the figures enhance the stillness.

Although the last shot of the piece returns to the little paper horse as it rotates on its thread, its implications are different from those of the opening shot. Gradually, it becomes clear that the horse's movement is slowing down until, just before it stills, the image fades to black. In the first instance, the slowing down relates to the gradual maturing of the child and his inevitable move out of the world of play and the imagination. But it also has a formal significance as, once again, thematic and formal threads weave together. The passage from movement to stillness evokes the stillness of 'the end' when a story or event that has been set into movement by an opening push, that carries forward into a sequence, begins to return to inertia. Ending with an image of stasis has a particular resonance for the moving image. While movement in a story is an effect of narrative, often in folk tales finding a figuration in the hero or heroine's journey, movement is the essential characteristic of cinema.

Here, to slow down, or to return to inertia, hints at an equivalent slowing down of the machine itself and threatens a crisis of representation. As the magic of the cinema begins to fade, it takes on a metaphoric dimension suggesting that endings tend to coincide with, or stand in for, human ends. Both the stilling of the image and the stilling of human life evoke an awareness of the filmstrip's own stillness and its closeness to the photographic image, with its own connotations of the past and the preservation of life after death. While the still photograph, or, indeed, a painting, can capture a movement in suspended animation, the cinema's destiny is to reanimate the inanimate, bringing it back to the illusion of movement, life and temporal duration. In Sutapa Biswas's *Birdsong*, the representation of time, its aesthetic and thematic dimensions, are examined but within a world that defies logic and creates a temporal and spatial framework of great beauty and complexity.

Two Places at Once, or the Same Place Twice: The Art of Sutapa Biswas

Ian Baucom

In Paul Muldoon's poem 'Twice', the Irish poet, who in recent years has emigrated from his native Ulster to the shady confines of an Ivy League American university, directs his readers to a photograph that in many ways allegorises the difficulties and pleasures of his transatlantic existence. The photo is from his childhood, a conventional classroom shot of a triple row of school-aged youths, smiling, or staring sullenly, at the lens of the camera. What distinguishes the photograph, what makes it both instantly memorable and, for the middle-aged poet, retrospectively symbolic of his and Ireland's experience of migrancy, is the grinning delinquency of one of the students, a boy named Lefty Clery, who gazes out at us 'from both ends of the school photograph,/having joked behind the three/deep rest of us to meet the Kodak's/leisurely pan; "Two places at once, was it, or one place twice?"'[01] Lefty's joke, as the question with which the poem responds to it indicates, is, like all good jokes, more complex than it first appears. It is a joke at the expense of the camera, or, more accurately, it is a taunting of the camera, a flaunting of the human capacity to outwit the memory devices we have created. The event, Lefty's shifting body testifies, exceeds our abilities to record it, or to remember it. But if history, even the mundane history of the school room, thus defies the authority and the competence of the archivist, it does so, this photograph suggests, not by making itself unavailable for study, but by depositing in the archive serial, and contradictory, images of itself. If Lefty's action thus mocks the pretensions of our memorialising tendencies and the competence of our technologies of memory, if it is, therefore, both a human joke and a joke about the work of art in an age of mechanical reproduction, then, for Muldoon, it is also a mournful joke, a joke about the traumas of colonial and postcolonial migrancy. In the Irish tradition of dancing at the wake, the smile that Muldoon returns to Lefty's trickery is forced. It represents a decision to satirise rather than to lament the realities of an imperial and post-imperial history which have required legions of Irish and Indian and African and Caribbean subjects to learn how to inhabit a space that, like Lefty's, is neither here nor there, neither Irish or American, neither English or Indian, but both, at once. As Muldoon knows, the real trick is, in fact, to learn how to inhabit that doubleness permanently, to learn what it means to occupy 'two places at once' after the camera has clicked. For this, of course, is Lefty's fate. Having mocked the camera for its pretensions on the truth he is himself mocked for his presumption. As the shutter closes it traps Lefty inside his joke, dooming him to stare out at the world from the same, split, place. Not once, or even twice, but each time that photograph is encountered.

Sutapa Biswas is not Irish, and her aesthetic, unlike Muldoon's, is not uninterruptedly satiric (though some of her early work, particularly a piece such as *The Only Good Indian...* (1985) which depicts an Indian woman meticulously carving the features of a Tory MP into a potato, is quite cuttingly satiric). But the territory she has charted as a photographer, a painter and an installation artist, is, like Muldoon's, a split territory, a transnational, trans-oceanic territory of belonging, a migrant and migrating territory in which, as Salman Rushdie has it, there is not one but 'many stories to tell, too many', in part because the subjects of this diasporic space are always travelling, whether in body, in memory, in imagination, or in desire, between here and there, now and then, the local and the global.[02] Biswas's work occupies and illuminates that travelling space. It does so by paying particular attention to the female subjects of the South Asian diaspora, by shuttling back and forth across the waters of empire to find the signs of life that a dispersed community of women has written onto its several landscapes of belonging.

In Biswas's work there is an element of anger, but also of aggressive pleasure, in what the artist finds and reveals to her audience, a combustible mix that is perhaps most evident in her celebrated 1985 work *Housewives with Steak-Knives*, a canvas which depicts Kali, the Hindu divinity of peace and of war, as one of the repeating household goddesses of the South Asian diaspora. The sensuous, muscular strength of this undomesticated wanderer, the glance of menace that she returns to all those who presume to run their eyes across her, is complicated, however, by the apparent physical fragility of the piece. Composed of sections of acrylic-, oil-, and pastel-covered paper, which were then glued on canvas, *Housewives with Steak-Knives* is a self-consuming artifact, a work that to its curators' horror is persistently dismantling itself as, moment by moment, it sheds its paper skin. But to read this self-defoliating canvas as a 'fragile' work, as one that requires its curators to protect it from itself, is a mistake (and a characteristically imperial mistake:

To Kill Two Birds with One Stone, 1994. Saris borrowed from Winnipeg, local stones, variable dimensions. Installation performance, Plug In Gallery, Winnipeg, Canada.

the British empire built itself on such patronising misunderstandings). For as the canvas unglues itself, it scatters Kali's body, distributing fragments of this female presence abroad. In so doing, Biswas's work allegorises the post-imperial scatterings of the women of the subcontinent. But it also insists that identity survives dispersal. It reminds us that identity, as Plutarch (an earlier subject of a globalising empire) observed, is something which always encounters itself 'in the middle of coming to be and passing away… it scatters and again gathers, or rather not again or afterwards but at the same time it comes together and flows away… approaches and departs.'[03]

In her later work, Biswas has continued to chart the ebb and flow of diasporic identity, though her idiom is now more frequently poignant, elegiac, or understated. This, certainly, is the idiom of *To Kill Two Birds with One Stone*, an exhibit she mounted at the Plug In Gallery in Winnipeg, Canada in 1993. For this show, Biswas borrowed twenty-eight saris from Indian and non-Indian Canadians, tagged these with tea-stained labels and arranged them in a floor sculpture. Gathered together, these textiles assumed the appearance of reciprocal 'gifts':[04] intimate gifts of

clothing collected from across the country and given to Biswas for use in the show, and gifts which Biswas returned to her audience simply by gathering them together, if only for a moment, before returning the saris and her audience (like the wandering strips of paper that momentarily compose the surface of *Housewives*) to their many different 'homes'.

On the walls of the Plug In Gallery, surrounding the sari floor sculpture, Biswas hung a sequence of black and white photographs from her 1992 exhibition *Synapse*. The reappearance of these images in *To Kill Two Birds* and in another 1992 work, *White Noise* (where, reprinted as transparencies and displayed in back-lit light boxes, they share wall space with an array of orange- and blue-toned winter landscapes), is characteristic of Biswas's interest in the aesthetics of repetition. As the social logic of diasporic cultural formations implies a spatialisation of the uncanny, the continual displacement and reappearance (in the joint sense of the word) of bodies, languages, visual symbols, narrative practices, forms of worship, styles of cooking, and modes of dress across ever wider spaces of the globe, so Biswas's diasporic art practice organises itself, in part, around the reappearance, the travelling,

60

Above left: *Frieze*, 1992. Black and white photographs mounted on MDF (multi-part work), 12m. Installation view, Yale University Art Gallery, 1998.

Above centre: *Synapse 1*, one, 1992. Black and white photograph, 112.2 x 132.5cm, Oldham City Art Gallery Collection, UK.

Above right: Rembrandt, *A Woman Bathing in a Stream (Hendrickje Stoffels?)*, 1654. Oil on oak, 61.8 x 47cm. © National Gallery, London.

of key images. Her art, like diaspora culture, is invigorated by the troping and re-troping of itself. One of Biswas's key images is of the female hand, which appears serially throughout her work: brandishing a knife in *Housewives*; carving in *The Only Good Indian…*; holding a cup in *Untitled (Woman in Blue Weeping)* (a 1996 video piece which, like so many of Biswas's works, re-creates a Western European 'masterpiece', in this case Vermeer's *Woman in Blue Reading a Letter*, c. 1662–63); soundlessly (clapping in several of the photographs in *Scarred Surface*, 1992, The Photographers' Gallery, London); and dipping into a body of water in the *Synapse I* and *Frieze* sequences from *Synapse* (1992, The Photographers' Gallery, London). A figure of the artist's making hand, and a figure, therefore, of figuration itself, the hand embodies not only the aesthetic per se but holds the aesthetic of dispersed identity which is Biswas's particular concern.

This is perhaps nowhere more clearly evident than in one of the images that compose *Synapse*, an image which reappears not precisely as the central image of *Frieze* (there is no 'centre' to that work), but as its serial organising principle. In the image itself (printed as a black and white photograph in *Synapse I*) two girls and a boy are standing in water, immersed to their knees, gazing directly at us.[05] Their bodies are neither perfectly relaxed nor rigidly tense. Rather, they hold themselves as if photographed by surprise, uncertain whether to dip their dangling hands into the water, to delight in the cool shallows, or to formalise themselves, to adopt a pose, to substitute decorum for the forgettable postures of play. Photographed an instant too late and an instant too soon, caught in a moment between abandon and self-collection, the three figures also wade between visual genres. The image implies a camera operator who may be an anthropologist, an artist, or a loved one. Either a snapshot for a family album, a study for gallery display, or a document for an ethnographic treatise, the photograph encloses the bathers in a multitude of literal and epistemological frames.

But if the undeveloped sandy beach and the wooded coastline invoke the anthropological at its primitivising worst, and the precise cropping of the image alludes to the primness of the gallery, then these innermost and outermost containing devices confront a third way of holding these individuals, an intermediate, memorialising frame. For, as we scan the shadowy space between the landscape

enclosing these untimely *baigneurs* and the mounted photograph's edge, we note the enveloping presence of another, unclad, female body. This fourth, barely visible figure, hands crossed at her waist, acts as a screen on to which the central image has been projected. Cradling this water scene, this woman obliges us to consider the figures broadcast on her body as something more than pieces of fieldwork or aesthetic artifacts, to view them also as the spectral inhabitants of a guardedly intimate, intra-uterine space. Positioned in a multitude of framing spaces, these figures, like the cultural locations they occupy, also inhabit a shifting series of moments. For if the gallery, the family album, and the anthropological treatise all too frequently 'make their objects' through acts of temporal displacement, through technologies of display which worship the pastness of the past, then the re-collection of these three persons in the womb of the fourth discloses these bathers as subjects not only of a then and a now but of a *yet-to-be*.[06] Perhaps, as Gilane Tawadros suggests, 'a remembrance of things past and present', the photograph is also a proleptic souvenir, a snapshot of the future reappearances of a diasporic community.[07] But if this image is a document of continuity, then it is

also, when it reappears in the seventy-nine panels of *Frieze*, a reminder that while identity may survive the traumas of displacement, it always re-creates itself with a difference. Serially repeated across the twelve-metre surfaces of *Frieze*, the image of these bathers is never identical from one panel to the next. It is not only that it is cropped differently, or that the panels are hung at different heights and different angles, but that in manually reproducing the images the artist never recreates an identical shading of light. The mechanics of reproduction, Biswas acknowledges, alter the thing reproduced. Each time it travels through her developing liquids, the image changes. It is subtly refashioned, as our bodies are marginally refashioned each time we immerse ourselves, as our identities are altered when we travel. This change is, of course, not entire or catastrophic. But it is real. Biswas makes no effort to hide this fact. In some of the panels, the viewer can even detect gridmarks, lines scored into the surface of the piece as it lay on the developing board. Stephen Greenblatt calls such marks signs of 'resonance',[08] signatures of history's estranging, damaging, renewing imprint stamped onto the work of art as it travels through space and time.

Above left: *Sacred Space*, 1990.
Black and white litho film and glass.
Installation view, Slade School of Art,
University College, London.

Above: *Sacred Space* (detail), 1990.
Black and white litho film and glass.
36.5 x 36.5cm.

Above left: *Sacred Space*, 1990.
Installation view, Slade School of Art,
University College, London.

Above right: Edward Hopper, *Sun in
an Empty Room*, 1963. Oil on canvas,
74.3 x 101.6cm. Private collection.
Photograph: Neil Greentree.

In Biswas's exploration of the aesthetics of diaspora, there is nothing shameful in such marks, no need to pretend that repetition has no room for difference, that the continuous is always marginally discontinuous with itself.

In the 1990 exhibit *Sacred Space*, mounted at the Slade School of Art, London University, Biswas used the flow of light to explore the doublings, translations, dispersals, and recollections of diaspora identity which she coded onto the paper skin of *Housewives*, realised in largely conceptual terms in *To Kill Two Birds*, and marked onto the non-coinciding surfaces of the panels of *Frieze*. Mounted in a room whose windows give on to a view of the School of Oriental and African Studies, the exhibit carefully manipulated the architecture and the lighting of that room. Opposite the windows, Biswas hung a series of black and white photographs, printed as transparencies and framed between planes of reflective glass. The images are of footprints in sand, enigmatic cryptograms of the human body which might remind the viewer of Crusoe's Friday, or, more innocuously, of a vacation at the beach, but which, whatever vanishing human presence they testify to, serve as tactile elegies of presence and loss – though what

has been present and what has been lost is left scrupulously unclear. The characteristic ambivalence of these images extends to our response to them. For we are by no means obliged to regard these footnotes to history mournfully. To mourn the vanishing of the human body which wrote its signature on these sands is, in fact, to commit ourselves to a portraitist's epistemology of the self, or perhaps to an imperial epistemology, to a preference for fixity, immutability, permanence. Perhaps we should, instead, delight in what frustrates us, celebrate the refusal of this walker to stand still, affirm that the wandering subjects of history are no less present for marking their presence as an endless passagework between one place and another.

To arrive at this moment of uncertainty, however, the images must be seen. An apparently simple task, but one whose secret difficulty and complexity Biswas intentionally heightened. For the visitor who stands too far back from the transparencies, the light flowing through the opposite windows imprints onto the glass panes in which the transparencies are cased a reflection of the view outside. From such a vantage, the panes act as a sort of mirror to the scene behind the viewer's back. What she or he sees is not

a series of footprints, but the Victorian facade of University College (a neighbour of the School of Oriental and African Studies), one of the great institutions of imperial learning, an institution in which the British empire deposited its knowledge of the cultures it conquered, governed, and studied. As the viewer moves closer to the transparencies he or she crosses an invisible line beyond which the external reflection disappears, and an imperial epistemology gives way to a migrant way of looking and knowing. To arrive at that perspective, the visitor must imitate, in advance, the actions of the photograph's subject: he or she must refuse to stand still, must walk away from the disciplinary factory of knowledge outside. As we realise this, the images in the transparencies also become mirror images, though now we find ourselves belatedly imitating these departing walkers, trying desperately to catch up with these individuals who have already had the wisdom to turn their backs on the British empire.

If *Sacred Space* thus offers the visitor a choice, if it invites us to realise that it is not one room but two, if it asks us to choose which view we prefer, which side of the line we wish to occupy, it also offers another option. We can stand on neither one side nor

the other but on the invisible meridian, on the border where the light flowing in and the light flowing out meet, and distort one another. From here, the viewer can see both views, both the architecture of empire and the route-works of migrancy. To stand here is to refuse to read culture, and history, and identity, as a competition of binary opposites; it is to refuse to censor one view of history in order to gain insight into another; it is to refuse to believe that we are ever either 'here' or 'there'; to insist that every 'single' cultural location is, at least, doubly occupied. But to stand here is also to refuse clarity, to surrender ourselves to visual static, to embrace a partial, uncertain, shifting point of view. Biswas intentionally gives her audience no direction. She does not tell us where to stand, or walk, or how to decide. She poses the question.

'Two places at once, was it, or one place twice?'

First published in *Crosscurrents: Krysninger*, exhibition catalogue, Oslo: Riksutstillinger, 1997.

Above left: Johannes Vermeer, *Woman in Blue Reading a Letter, c.* 1662–63. Oil on canvas, 46.5 x 39cm. © Rijksmuseum Amsterdam.

Above right: *Untitled (Woman in Blue Weeping)*, 1996. Video Projection. Still.

Notes
01_Paul Muldoon, *The Annals of Chile*, New York: Farrar, Strauss, Giroux, 1994, p. 12.
02_Salman Rushdie, *Midnight's Children*, London: Penguin Books, 1990, p. 4.
03_Cited in Heraclitus of Ephesus, *The Cosmic Fragments*, edited by G.S. Kirk, Cambridge: Cambridge University Press, 1954, p. 381.
04_See Sutapa Biswas, 'To Kill Two Birds with One Stone', in *Locus+ 1993–1996*, edited by Samantha Wilkinson, Newcastle-upon-Tyne: Locus+, 1996, pp. 34–37.
05_The composition of the image is reminiscent both of Indian miniatures and of Rembrandt's *A Woman Bathing in a Stream* (*Hendrickje Stoffels?*), 1654.
06_See Johannes Fabian, *Time and the Other: How Anthropology Makes Its Object*, New York: Columbia University Press, 1983.
07_Gilane Tawadros, 'Remembrance of Things Past and Present', in *Synapse: New Photographic Work by Sutapa Biswas*, exhibition catalogue, London and Leeds: The Photographers' Gallery and Leeds City Art Galleries, 1992, p. 4.
08_Stephen Greenblatt, 'Resonance and Wonder', in *Exhibiting Culture: The Poetics and Politics of Museum Display*, edited by Ivan Karp and Steven D. Lavine, Washington: Smithsonian Institution Press, 1991.

To Kill Two Birds with One Stone
Sutapa Biswas

Yoho Glacier, Canadian Rockies, 1914. Photograph: Byron Harmon. A postcard bought by the artist in 1990 and an early source of inspiration for her practice, in particular, for *Murmur*.

Question__I was born in India and came to Britain at the age of three and a half and am now thirty-four. What does this make me?
Answer__Human.

Question__I was born in India and educated in England. What does this make me?
Answer__Human.

Question__I was born human. What does this make me?
Answer__Human.

Question__I hear what you say, but can you hear me? What does this make you?
Answer__Human.

Refiguring Nature: Women in Landscape
I am never easy with the idea of an artist making a definitive statement about their own work, because for me it is the actual process of making art that is so important. This process for me is measured and weighed privately according to both external and internal experiences – a process that changes with time and is always shifting. If forced, I would say that my work is intended to be contemplative. Often ephemeral, it is like a garden in which we hear both ambient sounds and nothing.[01]

My infant years were spent in a rural region, and it is for this very simple reason, I believe, that I am drawn to large, open spaces. I arrived in England with my mother and siblings when I was three and a half years old. We left behind my adoptive grandmother, with whom, strangely enough, I had developed a strong maternal relationship. We joined my father, who had arrived ahead of us, travelling by ship for several weeks across oceans, seas, and even the Suez Canal. My recollections of this journey are vague, no doubt reinforced by the trauma of leaving what was then, for me, my home. All that I can vaguely recall was the fear I sensed in my mother as she kept me close to her side after the purser had voiced his desire to adopt me.

In thinking through this extraordinary and traumatic transition, the reasons for which are best left to another day, I realise that in hindsight I can't recall my mother ever having had any real choice in making the decision to move – she never actually chose to be displaced. As a point of interest in thinking back to my grandmother, she too had not

Above left and right: *Murmur*, 1993.
Video stills.

chosen to be displaced from her original homeland – the partition in India by the British saw to that one.

So here we were, women dislocated and following instruction from a paternal lineage.

The sense of loss is never easy to quantify. Not of India, but the loss of my adoptive grandmother. I wish I could remember her smell. But I can't, so I assign her memory to my imagination.

She is not always there. Only sometimes, as I sit eating the odd cheese sandwich, is she there, staring at me from the corner of an empty room.

And so my first recollection of a journey was at the age of three and a half. Crossing an ocean seems so far away now. And yet I am both drawn to and afraid of water. These last two sentences were first used in an absent performance I did in mid-winter in Winnipeg, Canada, in temperatures of minus twenty degrees Celsius.[02]

Celsius. Adjective. Designating or pertaining to the centigrade scale of temperature at which water freezes at nought degrees and boils at one hundred degrees under standard conditions.

If pushed, I would say that at present my work explores the intersection where landscape, gender and identity meet with art history.

As I sit in a classroom, I think of Diana. She always looks beautiful but nervous. She used to live behind Harrods. She once said that for her there was nothing quite like ice-skating in the autumn in Central Park. I heard that she once had quite a brilliant mind. Looking at the landscape of Thomas Gainsborough, I place two postcards together, the edges exactly aligned, so that the landscape from one is divided from the other only by a thin white edge. The skies in both paintings are dense with turbulent clouds. The sun breaks through in the distance. Mary Countess Howe lifts her skirt of lace. Her breasts heave even behind that lace. The flesh of her hands is blue with the cold.

There is no time like the present.

I like to walk, and in my mind I know the colours of that place. It is May. It is June. It is September. It is almost December. I feel both safe and vulnerable. I feel addicted. I keep going back in my mind to that place. To those places. Blue. Yellow and red. The blue is not the sky. It is the snow.

I know that place where the trees rise, and there is water. It draws me and I draw it. Water, water everywhere and not a drop to drink. Funny how a little beaver piss can ruin things. Each year at this time of year, I am there.

Synapse IV, 1991. Black and white photograph, 112.2 x 132.5cm.

We once pulled the car over to the kerb where we ate our fish and chips. Comfort food. The vinegar reeked so strong a swarm of black midges propelled themselves against the window. It was not funny.

I like some words. I like images, and I like objects. Perhaps this has something to do with the fact that I am partially deaf. I'm not sure, but I suppose it could be.

Mary Rose. It seems so strange to name a person after a ship that sank. I wonder if her parents knew.

Synapse is a metaphor. In anatomical terms it is a junction between two nerve cells or threadlike extremities, consisting of a minute gap (of unquantifiable dimension) between two specialised regions of cell surface, across which an impulse passes by diffusion of a neurotransmitter. Also, loosely, any junction between excitable cells by which an impulse may pass.

Stream. Noun. A flow of water; to run with liquid. Folded, stacked, starched. Brand new. Crossing an ocean seems so far away now. And yet I am both drawn to and afraid of water. How to weigh a sense of time. If one drops a stone in deep water, it still disappears.

Weigh. Verb. To measure.

Soluble. Adjective. Capable of being dissolved, of being solved.

Synapse is a metaphor. Synapse is a place where two people meet. Synapse is a place where two ideas meet. Synapse is a gap across which two people's ideas meet. Synapse is a place.

Quantity of sound. Volume. Noun. Sensation. Sensation caused in ear by vibration of surrounding air. Sound.

Synapse. A body of photographic work in which light plays an important part in creating the illusion of space.

When you look at *Synapse I* – five black-and-white images that are fairly large-scale, OK, larger than life – it is difficult to see the presence of the body at first glance. Only when one's eyes have adjusted can one begin to see its outline. In observing, the more you look, the more you can see. The shape of the body, the flesh, the nipple. In some of these images, the central projected image is more suspended in an apparent black void. It is more silent. A semiotic ghost. A disembodied pair of hands and image. A disembodied pair of hands that cradle an image which does not exist. The heat both soothes and burns my skin.

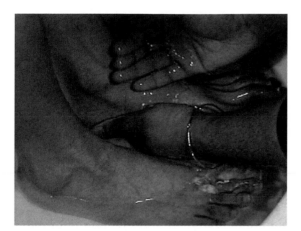

Murmur, 1993. Video still.

Synapse I, number 1. A line of trees rise up out of the water. Where are you? I only really know one of the people in this picture. Though all are familiar. Something burns to the upper right-hand side of the image. I do not know what, but the sky is more dense there. It's funny how your dress hugs your rounded body. The apocryphal heroine Susanna innocently aroused sexual desire in the old men who falsely accused her; Bathsheba's beauty (2 Samuel 10) tempted King David into mortal sin; seeing Diana bathing in the woods cost the hunter Actaeon his life.[03]

These are only some of the scars I find in this forest, where for me, because of the fire, it is both safe and unsafe. No less, I am overwhelmingly drawn to discover where you are. The light hits my body like your gaze, and, hidden behind foliage, I cannot see what you think. But you draw me like I draw you.

The projected images represent both imaginary and real spaces in both the mind of the viewer and of the subject. This paradox is accentuated through the interaction between the surface of the skin and the projected image – its interplay with light. Both the skin and the projected image work to interfere with, almost obliterate, each other. For me, this very process is a reminder of the way in which we recall a memory; vivid in places and, sometimes, meeting with blind spots.

…

Synapse I, number 2.

Question__I was born in India but England is my home. What does this make me?
Answer__Human.

Here in my studio in Canada, where I feel lucky with my suitcase, the walls are clean. The image does not exist, but still the light hit my body and burnt a hole.

Frieze. I nearly went insane making this piece. There in my darkroom, like some mad alchemist, up to my elbows in voodoo shit. Seventy-nine fragments. Seventy-nine fucking fragments. I was not pleasant to live with. It was a sort of hypnotic state. I placed the paper down and there in my space came an image I had seen before but had not quite recognised. Travelling from my darkroom in the basement to my studio on the second floor. Sometimes I would take the lift, but mainly I walked. Walking comes easy to me.

(I am rather attached to this piece, which when installed measures about twelve metres in length. It should be installed at an approximate eye level of

69

between 1.7 and 1.8 metres, the intention being that in viewing it the viewer experiences, momentarily, a strange feeling of submergence. The images move and shift like flickering pictures on an old super-8 film. The horizon line represents the edge of the world. The point against which all things are measured, according to nineteenth-century anthropological conventions.)

I travel to imaginary places where we meet occasionally. Where we are alone. We like to talk. My body feels soft and bruised, but really it is solid (*Synapse II*). The landscape is stretched and pulled like a bad/good dream. The horizon line curls and shifts, refusing me. I weigh myself against it. Against the edge of the world, which, as it undulates and ripples, breaks up nineteenth-century conventions. The fire is still ablaze, and the trees rise up out of the water. Sometimes I catch you in my hands, but you will not keep still. Diana, you always look so beautiful but strange in my dream. For each line that is made, another ten thousand can follow. The permutations are endless until there is only green bile. Sometimes you are not there and all that is visible is the gentle ebb and flow of the water. It feels like silence, and I am relieved that you have gone.

The land stretches and curls.

In her entry to the exhibition catalogue accompanying the exhibition *Synapse*, writer and critic Gilane Tawadros writes,

Memories are strange things. At times you can conjure them with a sleight of hand, like a magician, out of thin air. Others resist your effort to recollect and fall wilfully and persistently beyond your reach. Some memories can be invoked at will and fixed in space and time using all the paraphernalia of the past – old photographs, letters, souvenirs, family tales. Others are triggered involuntarily, vague recollections filtered through a smell, a sound or a glimpse of something in passing, yet which refuse to be anchored in a specific place or moment. Like a ghost sensed but never seen, the past haunts our present. We seize memories and grasp at vague recollections, impelled by our desire to map the journey which has brought us to here and now.[04]

Murmur. Noun. A rustling sound from the heart. I once went to see a doctor with an injured hand. He stuck pins in my skin from top to bottom and said,

Above left: Detail of one of the objects displayed beneath the photographs in *Scarred Surface.*

Above right: *White Noise*, 1992. Colour cibachrome. 26 x 21cm.

Notes

01__Artist's statement, *1996 Istanbul Biennale for Photography*, exhibition catalogue.
02__Performance commissioned by the organisation Locus+, Newcastle-upon-Tyne, England, and Plug In Gallery, Winnipeg, Canada, 1993. See *Vade Mecum*, Newcastle-upon-Tyne: Locus+, 1994.
03__See Erika Langmuir, *National Gallery Companion Guide*, London: National Gallery Publications, 1994, p. 228.
04__*Synapse: New Photographic Work by Sutapa Biswas,* exhibition catalogue, London and Leeds: The Photographers' Gallery and Leeds City Art Galleries, 1992.

'Tell me if it hurts, and describe the kind of pain it is.' Crossing an ocean seems so far away now, and yet I am still both drawn to and afraid of water.

Scarred Surface. Five large black-and-white photographs, each of which correspond to a photo-sculpture.

Clasped tight, no one can see what lies in those hands clasped tight, disembodied and suspended in a black void. All that is evident are the pressure points at the tips of the fingers. Mary Countess Howe with heaving breasts, your hands are so blue. Jute, wax, pin, stone, photograph, perspex, light. A landscape that disappears in the distance. As an X-ray it looks like pubic hair. Light hitting the surface of my stones suspended in air, makes shadows of my journey. Where do these stones come from? Scarred, scoured, eroded. If thrown into water one day, they would not exist, but perhaps for a grain of sand. Nothing stands still. Not even you.

…

Science. Noun. Middle English [of French from Latin *scientia*, knowledge; from *scient* – present participial stem of *scire*, know]. 1a State or fact of knowing; knowledge or cognisance of something specified or implied. And so on.

Nature. Noun. Middle English [Old and Modern (before language names) French from Latin *natura*, from nat – past participial stem of *nasci*, be born]. 1 The inherent or essential quality or constitution of a thing, the innate disposition or character of a person or animal or of humankind generally.

Somewhere between a rock and a stone.

Murmur. Noun. A rustling sound from the heart.

White Noise. Used to describe a place between radio stations. It is a garden.

And so I came full circle: to my blue ocean; to my fear of heights. I like to walk, and in my mind I know the colours of that place. It is May. It is June. It is September. It is almost December. I feel both safe and vulnerable. I feel addicted. I keep going back in my mind to that place. To those places. Blue. Yellow and red. The blue is not the sky. It is the snow.

Beth, I have never met you, and yet you sound so nice on the phone. You are an ocean or two away. This is my work.

May/June 1996

First published in *Camerawork: A Journal of Photographic Arts*, vol. 23, no. 2, Fall/Winter 1996, pp. 28–31.

Sutapa Biswas: Flights of Memory/Rites of Passage/Assertions of Culture A Five-Part Study [01]

Moira Roth

Enzo Biswas-Rodgers (left) and
Debidas Biswas (right). Photographs:
Sutapa Biswas.

'It is mostly about time and memory.'
Sutapa Biswas, 6 January 2004 [02]

1. The Evolutions of *Birdsong* and *Magnesium Bird*, 1997–2004

A Description, January 2004
'*Magnesium Bird* will begin as a… performance in Harewood's eighteenth-century walled garden when one hundred small birds sculpted from magnesium, connected to each other over a thirty square metre space, will be ignited at dusk. As an ephemeral piece of work, it will be intensely charged with themes of loss, love and trepidation. Documentary film and photographs of the event will be shown alongside a selection of bird drawings by J.M.W. Turner.'[03]

A Schedule, March 2004
Email from Biswas, 31 January 2004:
SB_*Magnesium Bird* is scheduled to be filmed on 20 March. In theory the actual filming should ideally be at the witching hour of dusk, which at that time of year we suspect will be around 4pm. In practice we will probably do several (three) takes before this time slot

on the day, as otherwise we may be cutting out our options should things not go according to plan. We will arrive the night before, on 19 March. I am hoping that six of my nieces and nephews will act in the work, plus Enzo, my son.

A Birth and a Death, 1997–2000
Enzo, Biswas's young son – who appears in her two recent films, *Birdsong* (2004) and *Untitled* (*Bit Part*) (1999–2003), and will be one of the children in *Magnesium Bird* – was born on 12 December 1997.

In August 1998, I attended Enzo's Naming Ceremony in London, a traditional Hindu rite of passage for young children which involves an array of symbolic presents and, most significantly, the child's choosing of one of these symbols to indicate his/her future. In a profound way – and, of course, given the complex resonances of the film, there are other readings of it – *Birdsong* is an amazing gift to a son from his artist-mother: a real horse, which satisfies the child's longing for such a thing, appears, as if by magic, in an elegant room.

On 26 February 2000, Debidas Biswas – the artist's much-beloved father, who was a distinguished Indian

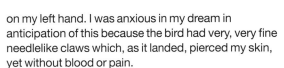

Above: J.M.W. Turner, *Jay*, from
The Farnley Book of Birds, *c*. 1816.
Pencil and watercolour on paper.
Collection Leeds Museums and
Galleries (City Art Gallery), UK.

Above right: Untitled sketches of birds,
2004. Pastel on paper, 29.6 x 21cm.

academic and intellectual, for years based in
London but still deeply connected to India – died.
She associates his death with birds and, more
generally, his life with gardens: 'He loved gardens and
was himself a gardener. He grew magnolias, camellias,
foxgloves, roses, cherry trees.'

Thus, *Magnesium Bird*, whose imagery is that of
the flight and death of metallic birds in an orchard,
accompanied by the play of lively young children,
clearly refers symbolically to the death of Biswas's
father and to the ongoing presence of her young son
in her life.

A Dream, January 2001
Email from Biswas, 20 January 2001:
SB__I've been having many thoughts around dreams,
some of which I had whilst in Oslo recently.

One night there I had a fantastic dream about a bird,
whose feathers were bright greenish-yellow. It was a
small, nervous bird, who kept jumping anxiously and
shaking its head left and right, before jumping to
another position. The strange thing was that every
time it jumped to a new point in my dream, it left an
incredible mantle behind made of traces of feathers,
coloured indigo blue. Eventually the small bird landed

on my left hand. I was anxious in my dream in
anticipation of this because the bird had very, very fine
needlelike claws which, as it landed, pierced my skin,
yet without blood or pain.

I thought I had dreamt about my father, and that he
was the bird, but perhaps it means other things too –
I don't know, as I'm still unravelling it.

A Statement by Biswas, March 2002 [04]
SB__My new research has arisen out of my having
become a mother in the last four years…. It probes
the psychological and emotional realms of such
experience… and I also draw on the writings of Marcel
Proust and Frantz Fanon…. The new work (some of
which is in the very early stages of making) are
multimedia based, and include video pieces,
drawings, a performance and a film…. The works take
the viewer through a metaphorical journey which maps
a set of human relations. These relations are bound
and severed by the very essence of human life:
birth; being a daughter and becoming a mother; the
transition from childhood to maturity; and ultimately
death and the loss of a parent. *Magnesium Bird* is an
ephemeral work; it is intensely charged, dealing with
loss, love, and trepidation.

Birds occupy a particular place in my consciousness, as they were the subject of the last conversation I had with my father before he died, and because the first sound which I heard after he died was birdsong.

Birds also occupy a great presence in life more generally because of their migratory existence. They are indicators of distance travelled, the seasons, the time of day, the subject of nursery rhymes (for example Edward Lear's *The Owl and the Pussycat*). Indeed they punctuate a sense of time and haunt us either in their presence or in their absence wherever we travel.

A Viewing, 31 December 2003
On New Year's Eve, I fly to London from California. Biswas picks me up at Heathrow, and we drive to her house, where I see on her television screen for the first time (after having heard about it over the last couple of years) the almost-finished, edited version of *Birdsong*.

Despite jet lag, I am totally mesmerised from start to finish. The double-screen film begins with the slow twisting and turning of an origami winged horse in front of a green-blue background (window panes through which one can see foliage). The scene shifts to an enraptured child (Enzo) as he looks curiously around,

this way and that, up and down, clearly scrutinising a presence that is at first invisible to me – though soon there appear tantalising glimpses of falling bridle reins and parts of a mysterious animal's body, shadowlike, passing in front of the child. Finally, after what seems to be an eternity (but in reality the whole film is just over seven minutes), a sumptuously furnished room comes into view, in which a large saddled horse manoeuvres around slowly. And so for the first time I understand the boy's intense curiosity. The film ends as it began, with the slow movements of the origami winged horse.

2. Visit to Harewood House, Yorkshire, 6 January 2004

A Train Journey from London to Leeds
Working on the train table in front of her, Biswas sits, absorbed, making a bird out of magnesium strip – which she plans to ignite later in the day at Harewood. She twists, turns and cuts the tape, weaving the narrow metal strips together until she slowly creates the full body of a glittering silver metallic bird with a long extended thin tail; although made out of a different material, the bird reminds me strongly of the origami horse in *Birdsong*.

Above left: Untitled sketch of bird, 2004. Ink on paper, 18.8 x 24.6cm.

Above right: Sutapa Biswas making a magnesium bird on the train to Leeds, 6 January 2004. Photograph: Moira Roth.

Test lighting a magnesium bird,
Harewood House, Yorkshire, UK,
6 January 2004. Photographs:
Moira Roth.

I take a series of photographs of Biswas; on one side of her is the window reflecting townscapes and the changing English landscape, and on the other side sits a companion in our journey, Bruce Haines from inIVA. Also travelling with us is Bevis Bowden (production co-ordinator to this project) from Film and Video Umbrella; Bowden will be doing the videotaping today.

The Country House of Harewood and Its Gardens
It is one of those impossibly lavish English estates with a formidable pedigree.

Harewood is recorded in the 1086 Domesday Book,[05] and by 1738 had been bought by the Lascelles family to whom it still belongs over two and a half centuries later; it is now set up as a trust and has recently opened to the public.

The house's foundations were laid in 1759, the architectural plans tinkered with by Robert Adams, and the house became occupied in 1771, fitted out with Chippendale furniture and decorative panels on the ceilings and walls by Angelica Kauffman and her contemporaries. In 1772 Capability Brown, the famous eighteenth-century landscape designer, submitted plans for its park. It is a site that conjures up for me the

art of Constable and Turner[06] as well as the poetry of Wordsworth and Crabbe.

Arriving at the grand front entrance of the house, we meet Sarah Brown, curator at The Culture Company who programme Harewood House, and stroll through the estate together (missing the Bird Garden, which at this time of year – winter – is closed), past the West and Woodland Gardens, along the Lakeside Walk, past the Rock Garden and Cascade, and through the greenhouse area, finally arriving at our destination: the Walled Garden. It is in this expanse of land, surrounded by a vine-encrusted brick wall, next to the Spiral Meadow, that we come across the orchard – the site of the forthcoming film – with its barren branches and stretches of well-tended ridged grass.

A Trial Run
We watch the test of what will be a complex spectacle in March – all of us, surely, trying to imagine the scene of many magnesium birds set on fire, interspersed with children gambolling in the orchard, which by March should be springlike with budding trees.

It is cold and windy, and we stand here, bundled in coats, scarves and gloves, while Biswas lays down in the grass the fragile silver-coloured bird she made

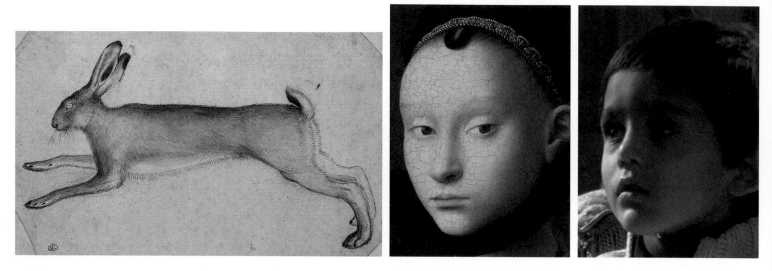

during the train ride. Haines then ignites it and Bowden films it on a small video camera with a monitor.

The single bird, poignantly small and alone, burns brightly, sending off trails of grey smoke. Finally all that remains is a molten metal corpse smouldering in the grass. (Biswas describes her memories of a funeral bier she once saw in the Ganges and of the sunlight beating down on the blue water of that river.)

Afterwards, Biswas and Bowden talk about the production plans for March. What angles does Biswas want for the scene? Should the camera move or not in order to track the event? There are to be several children. Where should they be situated? Sound? The ignition of the magnesium birds will be quiet, but the kids probably not. How to record this?

A Train Journey from Leeds to London
On the journey back (it is about two and a half hours from Leeds to London), Biswas shows me her current notebook. Stuck into it are postcards of paintings, including Petrus Christus's *Portrait of a Young Girl* (*c*. 1460) and Pisanello's *Running Hare* (1430–42) and sketches of Enzo's head and the room in which *Birdsong* was shot. The last sketch (of the Harewood orchard) was made earlier today.

We talk of films in the context of discussing why people make 'short' films (as Biswas does). She remarks that with most films, she tends to recall vividly only particular moments within the film, rather than the film as a whole, and these moments are what visually obsess her. She also relates that the first time she ever fell in love with a painting was when she was aged fourteen and saw Vermeer's *Woman in Blue Reading a Letter* (*c*. 1662–63).

3. Musings, Berkeley, California, 31 January 2004

I sit assembling my notes, reading through my diary, and looking at, over and over again, the clips from various video/film pieces that Biswas has done since 1993, on a videotape sent to me by inIVA[07] – all in preparation for an intense email exchange that Biswas and I have scheduled for tomorrow.

For me, what makes Biswas's work so extraordinary is its range of references and tones. Like some perfectly tuned musical instrument or voice, she can move elegantly and unexpectedly from a single long pitched note to an almost orchestral richness of sounds, from the melodic to the harsh, and from a dominant to a minor key and back.

Above left: Pisanello, *Running Hare*, 1430–32. Collection Musée du Louvre. © Photo RMN – C. Jean.

Above centre: Petrus Christus, *Portrait of a Young Girl* (detail), *c*. 1460. Staatliche Muzeen zu Berlin – Gemäldegalerie. © Bildarchiv Preussischer Kulturbesitz, Berlin. Photograph: Joerg P. Anders.

Above: *Birdsong* (detail), 2004. Film still.

Magnesium bird.

Above: The Walled Garden, Harewood House. Photograph: Moira Roth.

Above right: Sketch of the Walled Garden, Harewood House, 2004. Pencil on paper, 18.8 x 24.6cm.

I think back, too, on our Harewood visit. Of course, that house and its gardens conjure up delicious artistic and literary associations, but simultaneously more ominous ones, as it is the kind of site that inevitably evokes memories of the British empire, colonialism, and slavery.

In the 2003 Harewood House souvenir book, written by the Earl of Harewood, I read that 'by the late seventeenth century, the family's connection with Barbados and the sugar plantations they acquired there was firmly established.... It was the Barbados connection and the increase in the family fortunes which made possible the building of Harewood (my family only relinquished its links with Barbados in the 1970s).'[08] I recall Edward Said's subtle analysis of the shadowy presence of Barbados sugar plantation income in Jane Austen's *Mansfield Park*. And I think of what I know of references to such British imperial history and associations that thread their way through Biswas's work, from her undergraduate days at the University of Leeds and postgraduate studies at the Slade School, until the present.

I have always been impressed, indeed fascinated, by Biswas's unusual boldness when she was at Leeds. In 1981–82, Biswas had begun painting the outrageous *Housewives with Steak-Knives* [09] and, by 1984, at the age of twenty-two, she had staged a confrontational performance, in collaboration with Isabelle Tracey, for two of her instructors:

I invited John Tagg to come to my studio to view my work but he didn't realise that he was going to see a performance. He entered the room, and I invited him to sit on a chair and then drew a circle around him. After which we turned off the lights and bombarded him with prerecorded sound texts in other languages – in Bengali and Bantu taken from a black South African fringe-theatre activist group.... I wore a mask of Kali with clothing disguising my body, and then there was a small hand puppet which Isabelle held. A little later I invited Griselda Pollock to a more refined version of the piece.[10]

Already by this time (1984)[11] Biswas had studied Edward Said's *Orientalism* (1978), together with *The Empire Strikes Back: Race and Racism in 70s Britain* (1982, an anthology of writings on cultural politics by British-based Afro-Asian writers) and these early interests in postcolonial theory and the investigation of colonial history and practice have continued to deeply inform her work – witness the underlying references to such in *Birdsong* (2004) and *Magnesium Bird*.[12]

On one level, these two films are certainly, albeit in a subtle manner, about British imperial history and the legacy of that history, which Biswas has insistently, obsessively and inventively challenged over the years using various strategies and modes.

A major inspiration for *Birdsong* was George Stubbs' *Lord Holland and Lord Albemarle Shooting at Goodwood*, painted in 1759. Almost three hundred and fifty years after Stubbs painted this canvas, Biswas creates an extravagant, mysterious and bewitching film about a young half-Indian, half-English child who inhabits – for the fleeting duration of preparations for and the shooting of a seven-minute film, but perhaps also instilling in the child a lingering lifelong set of memories? – an elegant, carpeted room, carefully orchestrated in its colour scheme. The room's furniture and objects conjure up eighteenth- and nineteenth-century aristocratic and upper-middle-class English white culture – the culture, so to speak, of Harewood during these centuries (although any number of similarly historically laden sites might have been used). These associative details in *Birdsong* are combined with, indeed *counteracted* by, the child's toys, together with books and objects of personal significance to his artist-mother.

And the forthcoming *Magnesium Bird*? It is, on one level, a belated visual dirge about the departure, through death, of a beloved father; but the artist has chosen to stage the event, not in some anonymous forest, garden, or field, but in the walled garden of Harewood, a huge country estate in northern England with a rich and loaded history. One might, slightly fancifully, describe this as 'a walled garden of memories'.

It seems to me that Biswas is continuing certain interests explored in her early 1992 *Synapse* series (those marvellous large photographs of the artist's nude body onto which were projected images of Indian temples, peoples and landscapes). In a statement to accompany this exhibition, she explained that 'synapse' is a medical term for 'the anatomical relation of one nerve cell with another, the junction at which a nerve impulse is transferred, which is affected at various points by contact of their branching processes' and that the notion of synapse was 'a metaphor for the human condition with particular reference to the experience of memory'.[13]

In *Magnesium Bird* and *Birdsong*, these 'synapse' connections in the experience of memory take Biswas back and forth between the eighteenth and nineteenth centuries and the beginning of the twenty-first century, between colonial and postcolonial times.

4. An email exchange, London-Berkeley, 1 February 2004

MR__What attracts you as an artist/thinker to the subject/time period of eighteenth-century England? Stubbs painted his *Lord Holland and Lord Albemarle Shooting at Goodwood* in the same year (1759) as the foundation stone was laid for Harewood.

SB__Among other things is the fact that the eighteenth century marks the beginnings of the colonial relationship between India and England. For me the relationship is a complex one – about domination, control, exploitation, and more. But somewhere in this is a place where, in terms of 'discovery' (if I may be permitted to use that word rather lightly in this context), the meeting of two cultures went beyond the realm of what was permissible. A place where hate and love were rivals and at the same time two different sides of the same coin.

Rather than being fixed in this frame of the oppressor and the oppressed, I prefer to look at the overspill. To look at the place where in the complexity of these sets of relations and rules, individuals were perhaps able to feel that they belonged. One has only to walk around the old colonial quarters of Calcutta or Delhi today to feel that one is strangely comfortable with both forms of architecture, Indian and English. Indeed to be in love with both.

I encountered the painting by Stubbs over ten years ago, when I first embarked on a project that was to involve horses. I was looking at their portrayal not only in Stubbs' work but also in Constable, Gainsborough, miniature Indian paintings, even John Huston's film *The Misfits* (1961). Across all these various media, the horse represented an extremely charged animal. I have yet to analyse fully my fascination with this beast.[14] But it is there.

MR__I have several questions, too, about the conceptualising and making of *Birdsong*. How did you choose the furniture and objects for the set and where do they come from? What associations did you want to conjure up?

SB__In terms of furnishing the space, I initially set about considering a colour scheme for the room.

Since I had been trying, albeit in a subtle way, to reference Stubbs' painting, I thought that the most straightforward means for achieving that would be to simply use the same colours. I began by constructing a model of the room and decided, after examining a series of English Heritage paint swatch colours, on a colour scheme.[15] I chose a pea green colour (incidentally the same colour as the boat in Edward Lear's *The Owl and the Pussycat*). The ceiling would be white, and we set about trying to find furnishings to slowly build up the remaining tones/shades in the Stubbs painting.

I also began looking through my sketchbook, examining reproductions of various images and photographs I had collected over the years – all of which, as images, had haunted my psyche. I began to draw from them in terms of the general feeling and aesthetic I was after, for the film shots specifically and, more generally, for the space that Enzo and the horse would inhabit.

These images in my sketchbook included: a photograph of the interior of a restaurant in Rome, particularly the fireplace, which was quite plain and made from stone, and in many ways resembled the existing fireplace in the house of our location shoot in High Wycombe; Vermeer's *Woman in Blue Reading a Letter*; Petrus Christus's *Portrait of a Young Woman*; Pisanello's *Running Hare*; *Three-Master on a Stormy Sea* by Alfred Wallis (1930s); and *Landskip* (2000) by Simon Patterson.

What I love about all of these images is the incredible stillness of moment, despite the suggestion of movement. They all put forward a concept of time that embraces both the static presence of the painting and the inference in the painting of dynamic movement.

These two points seem to interchange to create a sense of rupture and disturbance. All of these images are exquisitely beautiful, which is important to me on an aesthetic and formal level.

Another image was Brion Gysin's *Dreamachine* (1960), which shows a man looking into the dream space of a magic lantern/carousel. The space behind the lantern reveals the image of the artist projected upside down, and it is unbelievably ghostlike. The idea of the *Dreamachine* is important as a juncture between the imagined and the real.

Once this general aesthetic was decided, we visited about ten prop houses looking for various objects which might sit comfortably in the context of the room.

Filming *Birdsong*, High Wycombe, UK,
October 2003. Location shots.
Photographs: Toby Glanville.

It was clear in my mind's eye that I wanted an authentic feel of a room that was inhabited. Yet I was not totally satisfied with our initial trawl.

We eventually were referred to a hire house and, upon entering, I knew immediately that this was exactly what I had been looking for. The furniture I chose included an Empire sofa and chairs; Empire lamps and shades; a large convex mirror (Victorian); two consoles (Napoleonic, I think); a cabinet and a bureau (both Victorian); two eighteenth-century paintings of a woman and a man; two small Victorian enamel paintings; a brass canon; a small Arc de Triomphe statue; the bust of a Greek goddess; a gold watch; ink well, etc.

I also brought with me several of Enzo's toys from home – among them, a plastic Peter Pan pirate ship (Disney); a small plastic rowing boat and oar (which for me refers back to my 1993 video piece *Murmur* and also to Lear's *The Owl and the Pussycat*); a plastic cowboy, horse and Indian; and several plastic Japanese robot toys – which lent a context in which we could move from the past (the period furniture) to the present.

Then there were books of my own, including: a book by Tolstoy, given to me by my father and containing an inscription to me; *Swann's Way*, the first volume of Proust's *In Search of Lost Time*; an anthology of essays by Jorge Luis Borges; a book on Vermeer; a book on Dutch artists of Delft; Derek Walcott's *Omerus*; a collection of Sylvia Plath's poems; and a book of poems for children by Robert Louis Stevenson.

I also brought with me and placed in the room: a photograph of my mother and father; a family photograph taken in Rome shortly after my father died; a photograph of Andy, my husband, as a small child; and a small paperweight containing the mature flower head of a dandelion, which I purchased at Kew Gardens several years ago. For me, dressing the room became as important as dressing a painting or a photograph. It became an archive of sorts.

Although the space was loaded with so much detail and so many references in the way that a room in someone's home is, essentially the situation allowed a complete immersion into that particular moment. In thinking about Robert Louis Stevenson, who once said that fiction is to man what play is to a child, I feel that the playfulness of creating the set allows the viewer to note the details but not be completely drawn away from what is taking place in the room at that moment.

In my previous email to you earlier this day, which disappeared into the ether, I was about to write about the work of E.M. Forster in the context of my fascination with the eighteenth and nineteenth centuries. In particular, *A Passage To India*, which I think is a remarkable and complex work. There lies in it an epiphany, a moment of the bright light of realisation. It addresses the complexity of the set of relations between empire and subject. It is brilliant in bringing into focus many sets of contradictions in terms of the accepted codes of behaviour of both coloniser and colonised, of unspoken desires and a natural sense of play and enquiry that is often forbidden by the rulers. Kipling, for example, was both of England and of India. Interestingly, as a young child, he was largely cared for by his *ayah* and his Hindu bearer Meeta and had to be reminded to speak in English when with his parents.

One of my earliest childhood memories is of watching films in a cinema and being carried home. Somehow, the bright light as it filtered through the darkened space held me, held my breath as indeed it held the particles of dust which floated through it.

Years later I reflected upon this when I watched *Amarcord*, a 1973 film by Federico Fellini, in which there is a moment when all the fairy fluff (plant seeds)

is released high into the air. It is an exquisite moment of rapture and contemplation. A moment when life and all expectations hang in the balance.[16]

In Proust's *Swann's Way*, which I began to read after my father's death, I am struck by the sheer suspension of time through the details of remembering. Somewhere between pain and a light promising new possibilities stands time.

I am unsure where Freud would place me if I were to sit on his couch. In many ways I would love to know what he would have made of it. At the end of the day, what I am left with is the sheer pleasure of just looking at and watching that moment of discovery, when in the stillness of time I see the impossibility of the moment come into being – an epiphany, a moment of bright light.

MR__I have begun to think about the concept of an epiphany and how it often (always?) relates to the way you initially conceive your work – such a dramatic contrast to the later, often highly time-consuming, making of that work.

I looked up 'epiphany' in my dictionary yesterday, and among the definitions found: 'a sudden manifestation of the essence or meaning of something' and 'a comprehension or perception

Origami birds given to the artist by Linda Ohama, a Japanese Canadian artist, as an auspicious parting gift following their collaboration on the exhibition *Memory and Desire*, Vancouver Art Gallery, 1991.

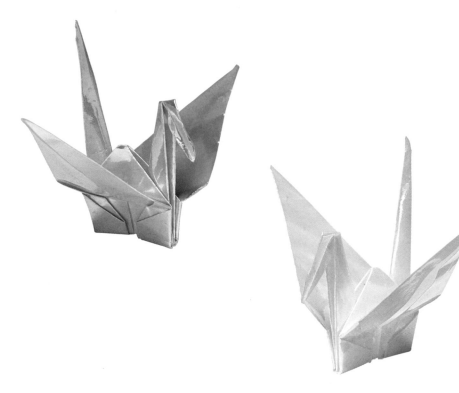

of reality by means of a sudden intuitive realisation'. It seems to me that this underlies *Magnesium Bird* in several ways, in its origin(s) and its making. The imagery of the piece has that sense of an epiphany for me: the sudden light change of day to dusk, the sudden fire/light of the ignited birds, the sudden burst of children running. Then (suddenly?) over.

SB__I had almost forgotten until recently the extent to which *Magnesium Bird* was a homage to my father. I think that for the sake of my sanity, after we had filmed *Birdsong* in October 2003, I put this a little to the back of my mind.

The last conversation I had with my father was about birds and about Proust and the millions of words he wrote. It is also true that there was a moment of epiphany at the time of my father's death, because after he had been pronounced dead, I arrived at the hospital and entered his room, and he came back to life and spoke to me and said in Bengali, 'Don't cry.' The first sounds I heard following my father's death were then birdsong.

I came up with the idea for *Magnesium Bird* after a dream I had in Oslo, in which I saw a bright fluorescent green bird hovering before my eyes. It was as a time when I was installing a work titled *To Kill Two Birds with*

One Stone, a reworking of a piece I first presented in Winnipeg, Canada. The dream was so vivid, very lucid, and haunted me for a long, long time.

The idea of an epiphany makes a great deal of sense to me and, as you observe, does perhaps relate to the way in which I initially conceive a work. It is also true that this is mostly in stark contrast to the very time-consuming way that an idea is then realised.

To me, the threads bringing these ideas together seem to be very much part of a continuum, in terms of seemingly eclectic sources of influences – like all these bits of a jigsaw, often from different puzzles, that fit together somehow.

Is it in keeping with how artists are supposed to make works? Should I be worried?

There is a great epiphany to *Magnesium Bird*; like a lucid dream, it appears, and haunts.

5. Musings, Hakone Gardens, Saratoga, California, 8 February 2004

I wake up early, lying on a tatami mat in a wooden building assembled a number of years ago in Kyoto and reinstalled here in this huge garden-park of some seven hectares with its Japanese bridge; pond with

carp, turtles, and ducks; and meticulously nurtured landscape, a blend of imported Japanese and indigenous Californian plants, flowers and trees. I look through the traditional screen windows and then walk outside. It is just after dawn and I can hear birds beginning to sing.

I wake up with the phrase 'a room and a garden' in my head, and realise I am thinking about (or perhaps had dreamt about?) *Birdsong* and *Magnesium Bird*.

I remember the sequence of *Birdsong*, that it begins and ends with the image of a window, and that *Magnesium Bird* is to take place in a garden whose walls are pierced with openings that reveal glimpses of fields on the other side.

Windows and walls? Inside and out?

In *Birdsong's* windowed room and *Magnesium Bird's* walled garden Biswas summons up notions of flights of memory, rites of passage, and assertions of culture. In these two spaces, Biswas has intermingled, almost with a sleight of hand, postcolonial and autobiographical associations and references. That's intriguing enough, but she goes further and interweaves mythology into this mix, as surely her birds and the horse bring to mind any number of magical creatures in Indian and European legends.

What's more, *both* Proust and Fanon appear among the artist's favourite reading matter. After all, Proust's notion which he writes about at the end of *Time Regained*, that time embodies 'past years, yet [is] not separated from us' and Fanon's commentary in *Black Skin/White Masks* that he must constantly remind himself that 'the real leap consists in introducing invention into existence' seem to haunt much of Biswas's work.

Biswas is an artist who, from the start, has brilliantly refused to stay put within a single theoretical, political, cultural, or psychoanalytic framework, or within a single historical time, or a single geographical place.

Standing in this Japanese garden in Northern California in the early spring of 2004, I wonder to myself: What surprising epiphany from Biswas will come next?

I imagine, in my mind's eye, that for a brief moment next month, during the staging of *Magnesium Bird*, the orchard at Harewood House will be transformed into a supernatural world of magical birds and mythic children, a world of fire and smoke, then 'ashes to ashes, dust to dust…'.

Above left: Sketch of an open window, 2003. Ink on paper, 14.7 x 10.2cm.

Above right: *Untitled*, 2003. Video still.

84

Filming *Magnesium Bird*,
Harewood House, 19 March 2004.
Location shots. Photographs: Jerry
Hardman-Jones.

Postscript: A Friendship

For years – ever since we first met in San Francisco in
1990 – Sutapa Biswas and I have been friends. We met
in the context of an exhibition, *Disputed Identities*, held
at San Francisco's Camerawork Gallery in 1990 – and
an accompanying panel that I moderated, in which she
participated ('Your Move or Mine? Perspectives on
Multicultural Photography, US/UK'). In the summer of
1991, I travelled to England and spent an illuminating
afternoon with Biswas, which I later described in an
essay on her:

> We sat for hours in an English pub talking
> about the empire, India, history, culture, race,
> and gender.... Biswas had grown increasingly
> impatient with the relentless stream of
> publications on the cultural and artistic impact of
> colonialism on India, regardless of the politically
> correct tone of the authors. A year ago she
> received a grant to research the influence of
> Indian art on the West.... We talked about
> cultural cross currents, cultural exchange and
> multiple cultural identities and homes, as well
> as cultural imperialism and postcolonialism.[17]

Since this time, we have continued to meet at each
other's homes in, respectively, London and Berkeley,
in restaurants and at exhibitions, to talk on the phone,
and to correspond sporadically (especially by email).
We have followed, with affection, and with political and
intellectual curiosity, each other's investigations and
flights of imagination.

Often I feel that we are fellow poets, although
occasionally – and this is one of those occasions –
I have felt like a critic-detective determined to get at
the 'truth of the matter', as I sift through Biswas's
brilliant fragments of elusive narrative, looking for
clues as to where the ideas came from and what they
'mean'. (I know, of course, that this is deplorably
unpostmodern of me.) Biswas is, however, an
excellent artist-critic-detective herself, and singularly
gifted in analysing her work as well as creating it.
As a result, our collaboration on this text has been,
I think for both of us, an interesting challenge and a
sweet extension of our friendship.

Above: *Magnesium Bird*, 2004.
Film stills, work in progress.

Right: *Magnesium Bird*, 2004.
Location shot. Photograph:
Jerry Hardman-Jones.

Notes

01__This essay is the eleventh in my *Travelling Companions/Fractured Worlds* series of texts, which I began in 1998. For a list of their titles and publication sites, see http://www.collegeart.org/caa/publications/AJ/artjournal.html

02__In an on-and-off conversation (from which I have drawn this quote) during our trip to Harewood House on 6 January 2004, Biswas talked about *Magnesium Bird* and other works. Unless otherwise noted, quotes by the artist are drawn from this conversation.

03__This description appears on the Harewood House web page (http://www.harewood.org/nav-shocked/index4.htm) and is based on publicity material supplied by the Institute of International Visual Arts (inIVA).

04__Excerpt from a grant proposal by the artist.

05__Commissioned by William the Conqueror, the Domesday Book was a huge land survey, assessing the extent of the land and resources owned in England at the time and the extent of the taxes that could be raised.

06__One of Turner's earliest patrons was Edward Viscount Lascelles, the owner of Harewood in the early nineteenth century. When *Magnesium Bird* is shown at Harewood, there are plans to borrow Turner watercolours of birds from the nearby Leeds City Art Gallery to install in a temporary exhibition at the house.

07__The tape that inIVA sent me contains either whole or partial scenes from *Murmur* (1993), *Untitled (Woman in Blue Weeping)* (1996), *Untitled (The Trials and Tribulations of Mickey Baker)* (1997), two short untitled fragments of a tablecloth and trees blowing in the wind (both 2003), and *Untitled (Bit Part)* (1999–2003) and *Birdsong* (2004).

08__*Harewood, Yorkshire: A Guide*, Leicester: Raitby Lawrence, 2003. p. 5.

09__*Housewives with Steak-Knives* was completed in 1985 for her Leeds graduating exhibition. In it, a Kali figure wears, as Brian Mulvihill writes, 'an English housewife's printed cotton frock with the traditional necklace of freshly severed heads (some bearing uncanny resemblances to Hitler, Trotsky and the former British prime minister Edward Heath)' (from *Sutapa Biswas: Synapse*, limited edition artist's book, 1991, p. 21; see footnote 17 of this essay). The woman stares out, wide-eyed and open-mouthed with tongue extended, and from her shoulders and lower body emerge four arms. She clutches various objects in three of her hands, and the fourth, palm extended, is stained with blood. In one hand she brandishes above her head a menacing steak-knife, and below she grasps the hair of the severed male head of Holofernes. The third hand holds a flower and a flag.

10__From 'A Narrative Chronology' in ibid, p. 23.

11__Also in the summer of 1984, Biswas began research on her undergraduate dissertation, 'Black Women Artists: One Hell of a Big Subject', and through this project met Lubaina Himid and Sonia Boyce. In 1985, she graduated from Leeds, and three of her works, among them *Housewives with Steak-Knives*, were included in *The Thin Black Line*, the now-legendary exhibition of eleven Afro-Asian women artists at the Institute of Contemporary Art, London.

**Untitled sketches of birds, 2004.
Pastel on paper, 29.6 x 21cm.**

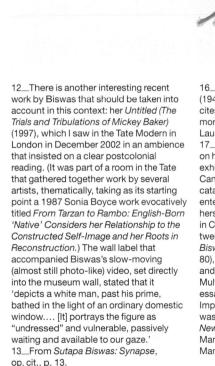

12__There is another interesting recent work by Biswas that should be taken into account in this context: her *Untitled (The Trials and Tribulations of Mickey Baker)* (1997), which I saw in the Tate Modern in London in December 2002 in an ambience that insisted on a clear postcolonial reading. (It was part of a room in the Tate that gathered together work by several artists, thematically, taking as its starting point a 1987 Sonia Boyce work evocatively titled *From Tarzan to Rambo: English-Born 'Native' Considers her Relationship to the Constructed Self-Image and her Roots in Reconstruction.*) The wall label that accompanied Biswas's slow-moving (almost still photo-like) video, set directly into the museum wall, stated that it 'depicts a white man, past his prime, bathed in the light of an ordinary domestic window…. [It] portrays the figure as "undressed" and vulnerable, passively waiting and available to our gaze.'

13__From *Sutapa Biswas: Synapse*, op. cit., p. 13.

14__When inIVA first released information about *Birdsong*, its title was listed interestingly enough as 'Beast'.

15__English Heritage is an official government body, which, since 1983, has been responsible for England's ancient monuments, listed buildings and conservation areas.

16__Jean Cocteau's *La Belle et La Bête* (1946) is another important film that Biswas cites in reference to her own practice. For a more detailed discussion of this film, see Laura Mulvey's essay in this book.

17__In October 1991, Biswas was at work on her *Synapse* series, which was to be exhibited at the Or Gallery in Vancouver, Canada. As there was no funding for a catalogue to accompany this show, she enterprisingly decided to create one herself, and in the context of this visited me in California. The result was a small, twenty-six-page artist's book titled *Sutapa Biswas: Synapse* (printed in an edition of 80), with vellum binding, Xerox images, and essays by Griselda Pollock, Brian Mulvihill and myself. Later, I revised my essay, 'Reading between the Lines: The Imprinted Spaces of Sutapa Biswas', and it was published in Katy Deepwell (ed.), *New Feminist Art Criticism*, New York and Manchester: St. Martin's Press and Manchester University Press, 1995.

Acknowledgments: I am deeply grateful, as always, to Michelle Piranio for her critical eye in reading the text, and to Sarah Campbell, of inIVA, for all her invaluable help.

Artist's Statement,
Sutapa Biswas, 2004

'Seeing, remembering and translating are all the acts of alchemy. Through time, the act of alchemy becomes apparent and revealed.

2004 – It has now been four years since I first drafted the proposals for what is currently coined as my new body of work. In this time, the work has come to fruition; the place of first proposals has been replaced by others, new and now in progress. And so time and motion sustain us.

1995 – At a conference titled 'Beautiful Translations' hosted at what was then called Tate Gallery, London, and is now Tate Britain, I first encountered the writer Derek Walcott. Walcott addressed the idea of translation with particular reference to Homer's *Odyssey* and its translation from the original Greek, to Latin, to English as spoken by Walcott's friend, a Barbadian whose accent Walcott likened to Elizabethan. Walcott spoke of "translation" in the context of the metronome, of sound: "I can't recall the words that we [Walcott and his Barbadian friend] used, but what I remember was the roll of the metre, the continual reproduction of that sound; to turn to a cliché, in the sustained reproduction of the rhythm, there was something of the [rhythm of the] sea; there was something of a sense of horizon." Like an adult who chanced upon a lost penny hidden under a carpet as a small child, Walcott's oral presentation left a deep impression on my psyche.

1996 – On a trip to Johannesburg (via Botswana), I was very kindly taken by an artist friend and scholar at Witts University, Colin Richards, to see the slag heaps left about the city from mining gold. After a day of also visiting the Soweto townships, where Colin was involved with various projects, I remember asking Colin as we climbed the acrid smelling slopes, when it was that he first thought about difference in terms of race. Colin (who is white Afrikaner, and grew up in a predominantly Dutch working-class area), told me a story of when he, as a very small boy, was playing with a young servant in his household – a small black boy. The two children were attacked by a swarm of bees. In attempting to run from their ferocious sting, Colin jumped into the safety of the water of a nearby pool, and called to his friend to do the same. The young black boy, too fearful of imprisonment for jumping into a "whites only" pool, didn't and as such sustained a fearful attack by the bees. Once the bees had passed, Colin turned to his young friend and helped him remove the stings from his body. Having witnessed his friend's traumatic experience, it was at that precise moment when Colin removed the bees caught in the young black boy's hair, that he realised difference.

2004 – For days after a pre-run test for *Magnesium Bird*, I felt that I could still see the retinal imprint left by the brightness of watching magnesium burning at mid-day. In the course of an eye test to check there was no damage, in the context of the central and peripheral field of vision, I came upon the word 'saccadic' for the first time. A brief rapid movement of the eye from one position of rest to another, whether voluntary or involuntary.

Looking, rhythm, translation.

There are some things in life that leave an indelible mark. These things are called up and drawn upon: the archive. *Riddles of the Sphinx*; the discovery and naming of Elephant Island; a travelling thunderstorm in a new place; a travelling thunderstorm in this place; a passage from Proust; a black painting by Barnett Newman; a white painting by Rauschenberg; my father's dying breath; Li Yuan-chia; Judith Mastai; a song sung by Danny Kaye about marigolds, a boomerang; Lewis Carroll; a secret.'

Artist's Biography

Biography

Born in Santinekethan, India (1962)
Lives and works in London

Member of Senate and Lecturer, University
    of Southampton
Lecturer, Chelsea College of Art, London
    Institute
Guest of Honour, Calhoun College, Yale
    University (1998)
Member, Board of Directors, inIVA
    (1994–96)
Fellow, Banff Center for the Arts, Canada
    (1992)

1995 MPhil, The Royal College
     of Art, London
1988–90
     Higher Diploma in Fine Art,
     The Slade School of Fine Art,
     University College, London
1981–85
     BA Hons, Fine Art,
     University of Leeds, UK

Awards and Prizes

Charlotte Townsend Award
Nominee, European Photography Award
    (1992)
Mark Turner Award

Residencies

2000 Art Gallery of Ontario, Toronto,
     Canada
1996 The Thapong International
     Workshop, Botswana (invitation
     from Robert Loder of the
     Triangle Trust)
1993 Western Front, Video and Media
     Production, Vancouver, Canada
     Locus+, Newcastle-upon-Tyne,
     hosted at Plug In Gallery, Winnipeg,
     Canada
1991 Vancouver Art Gallery, Vancouver,
     Canada

Selected Solo Exhibitions

2000 Art Gallery of Ontario, Canada
1994 Atlas Studio Space, London
1993 Plug In Gallery, Winnipeg, Canada
     Galerie OBORO, Montreal,
     Canada
     Synapse, City Art Gallery, Leeds, UK
1992 *Synapse*, The Photographer's
     Gallery, London (see exh. cat.)
     The Los Angeles Center for
     Photographic Studies,
     California, USA
1991 OR Gallery, Vancouver, Canada
1990 Banff Centre for the Arts,
     Alberta, Canada

Selected Group Exhibitions

2002 *From Tarzan to Rambo*,
     Tate Modern, London
2001 *Art Through the Eye of A Needle*,
     Henie Onstad Kunstsenter,
     Oslo, Norway (see exh. cat.)
1999 *The Crown Jewels*, Kampnagel,
     Hamburg, Germany (see exh. cat.)
     Identity and Environment,
     The Ludwig Museum of
     Contemporary Art, Budapest,
     Hungary (see exh. cat.)
1998 *The Unmapped Body: 3 Black
     British Artists*, Yale University Art
     Gallery, Connecticut, USA
     (see exh. cat.)
     Admissions of Identity, Sheffield
     Museums and Mappin Art Gallery,
     Sheffield, UK
1997 *Crosscurrents: Krysninger*,
     University Museum of Ethnography,
     Oslo, Norway (see exh. cat.)
     *Sexta Bienal de la Habana – el
     individuo e la memoria*, Havana,
     Cuba (see exh. cat.)
     Krishna the Divine Lover,
     Whitechapel Art Gallery, London
     Transforming the Crown, 1966–1996,
     Franklin H. Williams Cultural Center,
     New York (see exh. cat.)

1997 *MAPPA*, Amos Anderson Gallery,
     Helsinki, Finland (see exh. cat.)
1996 *The Visible and the Invisible:
     Representing the Body in
     Contemporary Art and Society*,
     site-specific works, University
     College London
     Divers' Memories, The Manchester
     Museum, UK
     The National Gallery, Botswana
1994 *Travelling Gallery*, Scotland (touring
     exhibition) *Beyond Destination*,
     Ikon Gallery, Birmingham, UK
     (see exh. cat.)
     Disrupted Borders, Arnolfini Gallery,
     Bristol, UK
     Expo Arte, Guadalajara, Mexico
1993 *Murmur*, Western Front,
     Vancouver, Canada
1992 *The European Photography Award*,
     Künstlerwerkstatt, Berlin, and
     Frankfurt, Germany (see exh. cat.)
     The Body Politic, Herter Art Gallery,
     University of Massachusetts,
     Amherst, USA (see exh. cat.)
     Memory and Desire, Vancouver
     Art Gallery, Canada (touring exhibition)
     Who do You Take Me For?,
     Museum of Modern Art,
     Brisbane, Australia

1992 *fine material for a dream…?*, Harris Museum and Art Gallery, Preston, UK (see exh. cat.)
1991 *The Circular Dance*, Arnolfini Gallery, Bristol, UK (see exh. cat.)
1990 *Disputed Identities*, Camerawork, San Francisco, California, USA (see exh. cat.)
1989 *Images of Women*, Leeds City Art Gallery, UK (see exh. cat.)
Intimate Distance, The Photographers' Gallery, London (see exh. cat.)
British Artists Abroad, Usher Gallery, Lincoln, UK
Fabled Territories, Leeds City Art Galleries and Viewpoint Gallery, Leeds, UK (see exh. cat.)
1988 *The Essential Black Art*, Chisenhale Gallery, London (see exh. cat.)
Critical Realism, Camden Arts Centre, London (see exh. cat.)
1987 *State of The Art: Ideas & Images in the 1980s*, ICA, London
1986 *The Issue of Painting*, AIR Gallery, London
Unrecorded Truths, The Elbow Room, London
1985 *The Thin Black Line*, ICA, London

Select Bibliography

2005 Ian Baucom, David A. Bailey and Sonia Boyce (eds), *Shades of Black: Assembling the 1980s. Black Arts in Postwar Britain*, Durham, NC: Duke University Press and inIVA
2004 Gil Perry (ed.), *Difference and Excess in Contemporary Art: The Visibility of Women's Practice*, Oxford: Blackwell Publishing
2001 Arts Review, *The New York Times*, 4 December
1999 Catherine King (ed.), *Views of Difference: Different Views in Art, Art and Its Histories*, New Haven and London: Yale University Press
Griselda Pollock, *Differencing the Canon, Feminist Desire and the Writing of Art Histories*, London: Routledge
1997 N. Poovaya-Smith, 'Keys to the Magic Kingdom' in *Cartwright Hall Art Gallery and its Collections*, Bradford: Cartwright Hall
1996 Sutapa Biswas, 'The Awakening Conscience', in J. Steyn (ed.), *Act 2, Art Criticism and Theory: Beautiful Translations*, London: Pluto Press
Sutapa Biswas, 'To Kill Two Birds with One Stone', in S. Wilkinson (ed.), *Locus+ 1993–96*, Newcastle: Locus+

1996 'To Kill Two Birds with One Stone', *Camerawork – A Journal of Photographic Arts. Refiguring Nature: Women in Landscape* issue, vol. 23, no. 2, Fall/Winter
Jonathan Harris, 'Visual Cultures in Opposition', in *Investigating Modern Art*, New Haven: Yale University Press
1995 Moira Roth, 'Reading Between the Lines: The Imprinted Spaces of Sutapa Biswas', in Katy Deepwell (ed.), *New Feminist Art Criticism*, New York and Manchester: Manchester University Press and St Martin's Press
'What's Critical about New Feminist Criticism? Griselda Pollock Asks of Katy Deepwell's New Book', *Women's Art Magazine*, no. 67, November/December
1994 Inderpal Grewal and Caren Kaplan (eds), *Scattered Hegemonies, Postmodernity and Transnational Feminist Practices*, Minneapolis: University of Minnesota Press
'Sutapa Biswas on Success', *Artists' Newsletter*, December
W. Furlong, *Audio Arts, Discourse and Practice in Contemporary Art*, London: Academy Editions

Left: Keith Piper, Sutapa Biswas, Shaheen Merali and Denise Bailey (left to right), *Shades of Black* **conference, Duke University, Durham, April 2001. Photograph: Janice Cheddie.**

Right above: Sutapa Biswas, Eddie Chamber's home in Bristol, UK, 1988. Photograph: Eddie Chambers.

Right below: Sutapa Biswas, Vancouver Island, Canada, 1993. Photograph: Andrew Rodgers.

1993 Sunil Gupta (ed.), *Disrupted Borders: An Intervention in Definitions of Boundaries*, London: Rivers Oram Press
Sean Cubitt, 'Beyond Destination', *Third Text*, no. 25, Winter
Griselda Pollock, 'Trouble in the Archives', *Women's Art Magazine*, no. 54, September/October
Gilane Tawadros, 'Sutapa Biswas: Remembrance of Things Past and Present', *Third Text*, no. 22, Spring

1992 *Synapse: New Photographic Work by Sutapa Biswas*, exhibition catalogue, London and Leeds: The Photographers' Gallery and Leeds City Art Galleries
Moira Roth in 'Two Women: The Collaboration of Pauline Cummins and Louise Walsh, or International Conversations among Women', *Sounding the Depths*, exh. cat., Dublin: Irish Museum of Modern Art
Ian Connolly Hunt, 'Sutapa Biswas: Synapse', *Art Monthly*, no. 162, December
Marina Benjamin, 'The Not so Naked Truth', *New Statesman*, November

1991 *Sutapa Biswas: Synapse*, limited edition artist's book, Vancouver: OR Gallery

1990 Janet Wolff, *Feminine Sentences: Essays on Women and Culture*, Oxford: Polity Press
Judith Wilson, 'What Are We doing Here?', *San Francisco Quarterly*, Fall
'Feminism in the 1990s, Sutapa Biswas', *Art Monthly*, no. 123, February

1989 Gilane Tawadros, 'Beyond The Boundary', *Third Text*, no. 8/9, Autumn/Winter
Miranda Strickland, 'Images of Women', *Artscribe*, October

1988 *The Massachusetts Review*, vol. XXIX, no.4
Homi K. Bhabha, Storms of The Heart, *Art Monthly*, no. 21, November
Arts Review, vol. XXXIX, no. 19

1987 Griselda Pollock and Rozsika Parker (eds), *Framing Feminism: Art and The Women's Movement, 1970–85*, London: Pandora Press
Hilary Robinson (ed), *Visibly Female: Feminism and Art Today. An Anthology*, London: Camden Press
Sandy Nairne, *State of The Art: Ideas & Images in the 1980s*, London: Chatto & Windus

1986 Sutapa Biswas, 'Tracing a History – Whatever Happened to Cricket', *Ten.8, Black Experiences* issue, no. 22
Sarah Kent, 'The Issue of Painting', *Time Out*, no. 840, 24 September – 1 October
Emmanuel Cooper, 'Images of Resistance', *The Tribune*, 19 September
Murdoch Lothian in *The Guardian*, 16 July
Waldemar Janusczak, 'Anger at Hand', *The Guardian*, 27 November

1985 *Artrage*, no. 11, Winter, front cover

Contributors' Biographies

Ian Baucom is an Associate Professor of English at Duke University, North Carolina. He is the author of *Out of Place: Englishness, Empire, and the Locations of Identity* (Princeton University Press, 1999) and *Specters of the Atlantic: Finance Capital, Slavery, and the Philosophy of History* (Duke University Press, forthcoming).

Guy Brett has written extensively for the art press and has organised a number of notable international exhibitions. He was Visual Arts Editor for the London weekly *City Limits* (1981–83) and Art Critic for *The Times* from 1964 to 1974. His most recent exhibitions, for which he also wrote catalogue essays, have been *Mindfields: Boris Gerrets* (Kiasma, Helsinki, 2002); *Li Yuan-chia* (Camden Arts Centre, London, and touring, 2001); and *Force Fields: Phases of the Kinetic* (MACBA, Barcelona and Hayward Gallery, London, 2000). His books include *Carnival of Perception: Selected Writings on Art* (inIVA, 2004); *Mona Hatoum* (Phaidon, 1997); *Exploding Galaxies: The Art of David Medalla* (Kala Press, 1995); *Transcontinental: Nine Latin American Artists* (Verso, 1990); and

Through Our Own Eyes: Popular Art and Modern History (New Society, 1986). He is presently writing a book on the art of Rose English.

Laura Mulvey is Professor of Film and Media Studies at Birkbeck College, University of London and former Director of the AHRB Centre for British Film and Television Studies. She has been writing about film and film theory since the mid-1970s. As reflected in her books *Visual and Other Pleasures* (Macmillan, 1989) and *Fetishism and Curiosity* (British Film Institute, 1996), her work has been influenced by and involved with feminism and psychoanalytic theory. She has also written *Citizen Kane* (BFI Classics series, 1996). In the late 1970s and early 1980s, Laura Mulvey co-directed six films with Peter Wollen including *Riddles of the Sphinx* (BFI, 1978) and *Frida Kahlo and Tina Modotti* (Arts Council, 1980). In 1991 she made a documentary, with artist/film-maker Mark Lewis, *Disgraced Monuments*, which was broadcast on Channel Four in 1994.

Griselda Pollock is Professor of Social and Critical Histories of Art and Director of the AHRB Centre for Cultural Analysis, Theory and History at the University of Leeds.

She has spent twenty-five years writing about and learning from women artists, developing feminist interventions in debates about cultural specificity and difference. Her recent texts include essays from the 1990s, *Looking Back to the Future: Essays on Art, Life and Death* (Routledge, 2000) and essays on women and time, Zoffany and India, Modigliani and Jewishness, and Charlotte Salomon.

Moira Roth was born and educated in England (London School of Economics), and then received a PhD from the University of California, Berkeley. She taught at the University of California, San Diego (1974–85) and now holds an endowed Chair in Art History at Mills College, Oakland. In 2000, she received the Frank Jewett Mather, Jr. Critic's Award (College Art Association). Roth has written extensively on contemporary art practice. In addition to many articles, Roth has edited a series of books, including *The Amazing Decade: Women and Performance Art in America* (Astro Artz, 1983) and *Rachel Rosenthal* (John Hopkins University Press, 1997). *Difference/Indifference: Musings on Postmodernism, Marcel Duchamp and John Cage* (G&B Arts International, 1998) is an anthology of her essays. Currently she is writing two series

of ongoing texts: 'Traveling Companions/Fractured Worlds' and 'The Library of Maps'. Among her 2002–3 theatre pieces are 'The Cyber Theater of Mneme (Memory) and Melete (Meditation)' and a play, 'From Vietnam to Hollywood' in collaboration with Dinh Q. Lê.

Stephanie Snyder is the Director and Chief Curator of the Douglas F. Cooley Memorial Art Gallery at Reed College in Portland, Oregon. Snyder's curatorial projects include *Bibliocosmos* (Reed College, 2003); *Film Show* (San Francisco Arts Commission, Reed College, 2003); *Being and Belonging: Reflections on Jewish Space* (San Diego Center for Jewish Culture, 2003); and *Performing Judaism* (Reed College, 2002). She is currently curating a solo exhibition of the work of Mona Hatoum for the Cooley Gallery, opening in 2005. An accomplished artist, Snyder has exhibited her work throughout the United States at spaces such as ABC NoRio (NYC), the Brecht Forum (NYC), the Vortex Gallery (San Francisco), and SUNY Stony Brook (NY). Snyder had her first solo museum exhibition at the Contemporary Jewish Museum, San Francisco, in January of 2003. Her work will be featured in the upcoming exhibition *Monument Recall* (SF Camerawork, October 2004).

Artist's Acknowledgments

The publication of this monograph on the occasion of the exhibition *Birdsong*, would not have been possible, were it not for the support, patience and practical help of many generous individuals.

In particular, I would like first of all to thank my late father, Debidas Biswas, without whose optimism and intellect, I would never have become an artist in the first place. I am also in deep gratitude to my mother Geeta Rani Biswas, whose patience and love sustained us.

I am indebted to Stuart Hall, for his kindness and unfaltering inspiration and presence over many years, and for his encouragement in my realising these new works. Special thanks go to Moira Roth, Guy Brett, Laura Mulvey, and to Stephanie Snyder. I am truly grateful for their generous dialogue; their commitment; and the time which they afforded me, and this project. For encouragement over many years, and their contribution to this book, my thanks to Griselda Pollock and to Ian Baucom.

My special thanks to Sarah Campbell for her professionalism and for tireless effort in editing this monograph and to Glenn Howard for his thoughtful design. I am grateful to Louise Bourgeois, the Comité Cocteau and all those who have kindly lent images for the book. For their support and belief in my work, my thanks go to Gilane Tawadros, and to Steven Bode. My thanks also to: Bruce Haines for his enthusiasm and good nature; David A. Bailey for his support and encouragement; Janice Cheddie, for all her intelligent dialogue; Lissa Kinnaer; Melanie Keen; Marcus Verhagen; Stephen Foster; James Lingwood; Rosie Miles; Toshio Watanabe; Gavin Jantjes; Jo Bruton. Many thanks to Sonia Boyce for her conversation and friendship. My thanks also to Sarah Brown, Deborah Dean and Ron Henocq, who have shown great support from the outset.

The making of my new film works has been a pleasurable journey; and there are many people to whom I am grateful. In particular, I am deeply indebted to Bevis Bowden for his insight and intellect, his generosity, and his sheer professionalism. To Nina Ernst, for her wit and generosity; to Teddy Testar, for his brilliance; Anna Vass; Helen Dowling; Kirstie Williams; Bob Hollow; Mike Jones; Caroline Smith; Keith Whittle; Rahoul Biswas-Hawkes; Aparna Biswas; Debjani Biswas-Hawkes; Sudipto Biswas; Maya and Uma Biswas-Whittaker; and all at Harewood House.

Being an artist is a tough job (apologies to coal miners out there, my husband keeps reminding me), but it is often an even tougher job for those around who love you, and who carry you through the best and through the worst. In this my deepest gratitude goes to Andrew Rodgers; Enzo Biswas-Rodgers; Deepa Biswas-Hawkes; and Sujata Biswas-Whittaker.

Birdsong Credits

Cast: Enzo Biswas-Rodgers, Rahoul Biswas-Hawkes

Crew
Artist/Director: Sutapa Biswas
Production Co-ordinator: Bevis Bowden
Project Co-ordinator: Nina Ernst
Cinematography: Teddy Testar
First Camera Assistant: Alex Taylor
Second Camera Assistant: Adam Roberts
Gaffer: Colin Field
Sound Recordist: Keith Branch
Animal Co-ordinator: Tanya Steele
Head Horse Trainer: Tom Strutter
Horse Trainer: Camilla Naprous
Assistant to Sutapa Biswas: Anna Vass
Chaperone: Pernille Leggat Ramfelt
Production Assistant: Alistair Whyte
Production Assistant: Helen Dowling
Production Assistant: Kirstie Williams
Offline Editor: Bevis Bowden, Film and Video Umbrella
Colourist: Rob Pizzy, One Post
Online Editor: Mark Wickens, Frontline Television
Produced by: Film and Video Umbrella
Location Finder: Location Works
Horses provided by: Rona Brown & Associates
Lighting provided by: AFM
Processing: Technicolor
DVD Authoring: Dubbs
Stills Photographer: Toby Glanville

Magnesium Bird Credits

Cast: Debjani & Rahoul Biswas-Hawkes, Aparna & Sudipto Biswas, Enzo Biswas-Rodgers, Maya and Uma Whittaker

Crew
Artist/Director: Sutapa Biswas
Production Co-ordinator: Bruce Haines
Cinematography: Bevis Bowden
Special Effects Co-ordinator: Bob Hollow
Special Effects Co-ordinator: Mark McKendry
Grip: Mark Bell
Production Assistant: Anna Vass
Production Assistant: Helen Dowling
Production Assistant: Kirstie Williams
Production Assistant: Lissa Kinnaer
Production Assistant: William Trevelyan
Location Manager: Sarah Brown, The Culture Company
Editor: Bevis Bowden, Film and Video Umbrella
Produced by: Institute of International Visual Arts (inIVA)
Special Effects: Bob Hollow Special Effects
Grip Equipment: ProVision Facilities Ltd
DVD Authoring: Dubbs
Stills Photographer: Jerry Hardman-Jones